Victorian Houses

Victorian Houses
and their details

The role of publications in their building and decoration

Helen C. Long

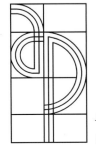

Architectural Press

OXFORD   AUCKLAND   BOSTON   JOHANNESBURG   MELBOURNE   NEW DELHI

Architectural Press
An imprint of Butterworth-Heinemann
Linacre House, Jordan Hill, Oxford OX2 8DP
225 Wildwood Avenue, Woburn, MA 01801-2041
A division of Reed Educational and Professional Publishing Ltd

℞ A member of the Reed Elsevier plc group

First published 2002

British Library Cataloguing in Publication Data

A catalogue record for this book is available from the British Library

Library of Congress Cataloguing in Publication Data

A catalogue record for this book is available from the Library of Congress

ISBN 0 7506 4848 1

For information on all Architectural Press publications
visit our website at www.architecturalpress.com

Produced and typeset by Gray Publishing, Tunbridge Wells, Kent
Printed and bound in Great Britain

Contents

Preface   vii

Acknowledgements   ix

Chapter 1   Introduction   1

Building Victorian Houses   2

The Publishing World   10

Chapter 2   Architectural Pattern Books and Manuals for Victorian Houses   23

Early Models   23

Architectural Pattern Books and Manuals 1820–50   26

The 1850s and 1860s   42

Architectural Books 1870–1901   59

Chapter 3   Pattern Books and Manuals of Victorian Exterior and Interior Details   71

Pattern Books of Designs   71

Trade Manuals and Price Books   76

Decoration and Home Manuals   88

Chapter 4   Trade Catalogues and Journals   97

Trade catalogues   97

Journals of Architecture, Building Trades and Home Furnishing   109

Postscript   121

Bibliography   123

Index   127

For Max

Preface

This book examines the publications that contributed to the making of small-to medium-sized Victorian houses and their details. Pattern books of house designs and interior and exterior detailing, manuals, price books, trade catalogues and journals, were useful sources of information for the architectural and building trades and the public alike, and played an important role in the transmission of taste and practical advice.

Supplementing the body of knowledge already available on the history of building publications, the book does not seek to provide an exhaustive list of all titles issued, but using selected examples, to construct a picture of the types of publications, their development and use. A discussion of publications relating to Victorian housing necessarily involves looking at works well prior to 1837, as their roots go back into the eighteenth century and early nineteenth century. The distinction between the Victorian period and what went before is further blurred and complicated by the fact that some early nineteenth-century writers' works were republished well into the Victorian period.

The book begins by briefly considering the building and publishing worlds, to show how changes which took place in the Victorian period impacted on housebuilding and its literature. The chapters following the Introduction look at selected publications in more detail, Chapters 2 and 3 covering pattern books and manuals, and Chapter 4, trade catalogues and journals. While designs for whole houses are covered mainly in Chapter 2, and house details in Chapter 3, there is inevitably some overlap in cases where books, journals and trade catalogues cover both total designs and details. I have divided chapters according to publication types as the most straightforward means of presenting material.

The strong visual emphasis of this book is intended to provide a vivid pictorial history supporting the text, in a sense, a pattern book of pattern books. The value of such a book, which points in the direction of all kinds of sources, is as a resource for a wide range of interested readers, Victorian home-owners and scholars in a number of fields.

Acknowledgements

First, I would like to thank The Arts and Humanities Research Board and The University of Wales Institute, Cardiff for enabling me to complete this work. Special thanks also go to Tim Coward, Katherine Reeve, Sarah Richards, Nigel Whiteley, and The William De Morgan Foundation (Jon Catleugh) for their help and support. I would like to thank my colleagues, Glyn Jones, Martin Gaughan, Steve Gill, Jenny Godfrey, Gill St John Griffiths, Arwen Thomas, and in particular, Kevin Edge and Megan Ngoumtsa. Thanks are also due to V & A Picture Library (Martin Durrant and Rachel Lloyd), RIBA Library (Robert Elwall), Cyfarthfa Castle Art Gallery and Museum (Claire Dovey-Evans), and in particular, Stephen Astley at Sir John Soane's Museum, Sylvia Harris at The Architectural Resource Centre, Cardiff University, and Matthew Williams at Cardiff Castle. Others have helped greatly, notably, Christopher Christie, Judy Cligman, Nancy Sheiry Glaister, Lesley Gray, Sue Hunt, Alex Jackson-Long, Chris James, David Long, Joyce and Ken Long, Ben Piper, Alison Yates and in particular, Tom Piper.

1 Introduction

The year of Queen Victoria's accession to the throne saw the publication of a range of new and reissued works, some of which demonstrated the continuum between needs and interests of the early Victorian period and the years prior to it, and others which highlighted issues which became prominent Victorian concerns.

Peter Frederick Robinson's penultimate book, *Domestic Architecture in the Tudor Style*, and Peter Nicholson's final work, *A Treatise on Projection, with a Complete System of Isometric Drawing* were both published in 1837. Reissues in 1837 of earlier works by these authors also dominated architectural publications for that year. Nicholson and Robinson were among the most significant and prolific writers on architecture and building of the early nineteenth century and, although they are technically speaking pre-Victorian, their influence, partly through the many later editions of their works, lasted well into the Victorian period; Robinson's pattern books of cottages and villa designs still influenced housebuilders in the 1850s and even 1860s, whilst Nicholson's practical manuals on a wide range of subjects, particularly carpentry and joinery, dominated building practice through the first half of the nineteenth century. Other books published in 1837 included A.W.N. Pugin's *Details of Antient Timber Houses*, one of a number of books by Pugin which set the foundations for rules on correct Gothic style, and C.J. Richardson's *Observations*, which provided a basis for accurate Elizabethan and Jacobean architecture. James Collis' *The Builders' Portfolio of Street Architecture,* 1837, was the first pattern book to be mainly devoted to terraced housing,[1] looking forward to the Victorian era of suburban housebuilding for the masses. Charles Hood's *A Practical Treatise on Warming Buildings*, 1837, in its sixth edition by 1885, highlighted domestic heating, which became a much-debated issue among professionals and the public throughout the Victorian period.

In 1837, a number of elements important for housebuilding in the rest of the Victorian period were in place. Key sources for those about to build – the pattern book, manual and price book – and which were to be important for building and decoration for the rest of the century, were established by then; but new types of publications were also developing fast, namely, the architectural magazine and the trade catalogue, which ultimately replaced many earlier forms of advice. Also by 1837 the basis of all techniques of illustration used in the nineteenth century were present, and organizational and technological change in the publishing trade was about to transform the scale and face of book production. The architectural and building world, too, was in 1837 in a transitional phase, becoming thereafter increasingly specialized and diversified, with new forces such as mechanization and transportation impacting on established ways of doing things. The speculative builder, the availability of a large workforce of cheap, skilled and unskilled labour, and of cheap machine-made building requisites, were of vital importance for the building and ornamental detailing of small- to medium-sized Victorian houses. Such changes were reflected across the range of publications dealt with in this book.

Publications for the year 1901 included Barry Parker and Raymond Unwin's important book *The Art of Building a Home*. Style had come full circle since 1837, from the cottages of Robinson, via E.W. Nesfield and others, to the Arts and Crafts ideal of C.A. Voysey, M.H. Baillie Scott and Parker and Unwin.

BUILDING VICTORIAN HOUSES

The population of England and Wales rose from approximately nine million in 1801, to 16 million in 1841, to 36 million by 1911, and the numbers of houses built rose from 1.6 million in 1801, to three million in 1841 to 7.6 million by 1911.[2] Peaks of building activity occurred in the late 1860s, mid to late 1870s and around 1900, with small booms in the 1830s, 1840s and early 1850s.[3]

Architecture became more formalized into a profession in the 1840s with the foundation of The Institute of British Architects, 1834 (Royal Institute of British Architects, 1837) and the Architectural Association, 1847. The number of architects rose to 3843 in 1861 and to 6898 in 1881, followed by a proportionally smaller rise by 1901. Quantity surveying and civil engineering also emerged as distinct spheres of activity, with proportionally similar advances in members, to 6414 and 11,052 (includes mining engineers), respectively, by 1901.[4] Architects became less involved in housebuilding and materials manufacture, these functions separating off with their own specialists. Old systems of calculating work as it proceeded, and the client making separate contracts with various trades, were increasingly controlled, either by using estimates and contracts where large houses were concerned, or, in the case of speculative building with no specific client, through building legislation, bye-laws, restrictive covenants and credit terms for speculative building.[5] Thomas Cubitt was largely responsible for developing the modern speculative building firm from 1815, where he employed all trades, foremen and financial staff, and manufactured his own materials and components at his works; by 1828, he employed 1000 men.[6] Cubitt built many houses in London, notably high-quality housing in Bloomsbury and Belgravia, and smaller houses in Barnsbury.

> 'A very few years ago Willesden was a quiet, retired, thoroughly rural village, a favourite haunt of the holiday-maker, summer rambler, botanist, and sketcher … The builder has invaded the once-tranquil meadows.' (Thorne 1876).[7]

Suburbia was essentially a product of the period 1815–1939, a response to demand for houses out of increasingly crowded cities. In 1839, S.H. Brookes said in the preface of *Designs for Villa and Cottage Architecture*:

> 'An Englishmen when he first travels on the Continent … particularly remarks … on the comparatively small number of suburban villas which are seen in the vicinity of even the largest towns, and which form such a delightful feature in the landscape scenery of England. … Par eminence, England becomes the country of suburban villas'.

By 1881 W.S. Clarke listed 89 suburbs of London. The demand for small suburban houses for workers prompted a new type of builder, the 'superior artisan',[8] to become involved in housebuilding in the so-called artisan suburbs of the 1870s and beyond. The origins of this class of building lie in the estates

NORTH SIDE. BELGRAVE SQUARE
PIMLICO

Drawn by T.H. Shepherd

Figure 1
North side, Belgrave Square illustrated by T.H. Shepherd in 1834.

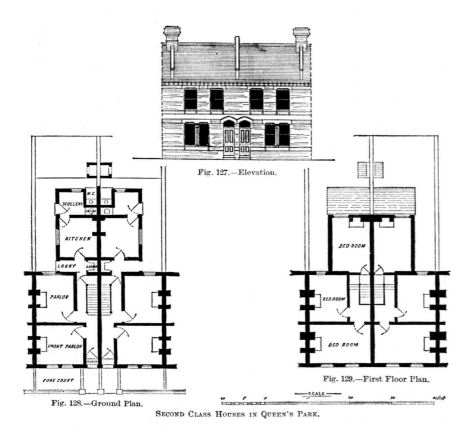

Fig. 127.—Elevation.

Fig. 128.—Ground Plan.

Fig. 129.—First Floor Plan.

SECOND CLASS HOUSES IN QUEEN'S PARK.

Figure 2
Second-class houses in Queen's Park with two parlours and three bedrooms on a 75-acre site with weekly rents of 6s to 13s 6d for three house types. Small suburban houses such as these were in very great demand by the 1880s.

of houses built by the semi-philanthropic Artisans and Labourers General Dwellings Company, founded 1867 by William Austin, who was illiterate, and started his working life on a farm scaring birds for 1d a day.[9] The first of these estates was such as the Shaftesbury Estate, Battersea, London, 1872, followed by estates at Queen's Park (Figure 2), Noel Park, and Leigham Court, London, and others in Liverpool, Gosport, Leeds, Salford and Birmingham.

Large-scale speculative builders, such as Charles Freake and John Spicer followed Cubitt in London's development in the 1850s and 1860s, and the trend generally across the country was towards fewer, larger housebuilding firms by the Edwardian period, but broadly speaking, the size of the average building firm remained small throughout the Victorian period. In north Kensington in 1845, for example, 31 firms put up 137 houses,[10] and in Camberwell between 1878 and 1880, 416 builders put up 1670 houses.[11]

The number of people involved in the building trades rose from 203,000 in 1831 to 497,000 in 1851, to 831,394 by 1881 and to 1,130,425 by 1901.[12] Paralleling increasing specialization and expansion in other aspects of architecture and building, individual crafts became increasingly hierarchically organized, with clearly defined boundaries between and levels within trades. New trades, such as the interior decorator and electrician, added to the ranks of the crafts involved in housebuilding towards the end of the century. The average building wage in 1860 was 32s a week, so building workers were well off compared to some other working groups; the cost of labour rose more than the cost of materials over the century.

Building materials supply shifted from the use of local materials and components made on site, to cheap offsite manufacture and imported goods. The repeal of taxes on materials like glass, bricks and tiles in the 1840s and 1850s also reduced costs, and made the bay window, and polychromatic brickwork, so typical of Victorian houses, economically possible. The builders merchant boomed after 1870, with its trade catalogues and credit terms, and provided fast delivery of ready-made building requisites. The availability of ready-made components, and of a large skilled and unskilled workforce for all the necessary trades, along with written advice for builders and others, and the increasing middle classes and standard of living by the end of the Victorian period, resulted in vast numbers of small- to medium-sized detached, semi-detached and terraced houses, resulting at once in homogeneity yet numerous varied combinations of details.[14]

In terms of styles used for housebuilding, architects and builders of villas could broadly follow styles in fashion for large country houses such as those by C. Barry, A. Salvin and A. Waterhouse, in vastly scaled-down and altered form, for so-called Italianate, Elizabethan, Old English, Scotch Baronial, French Gothic and so on, were all available in architectural pattern books of the time. Other models provided by well-known architects were also influential, such as the small suburban detached house and garden ideal influenced by John Nash, popularizer of the picturesque cottage and Italianate villa, at Regent's Park (Figure 6).

Figure 3
Carpenter's work, 1842.

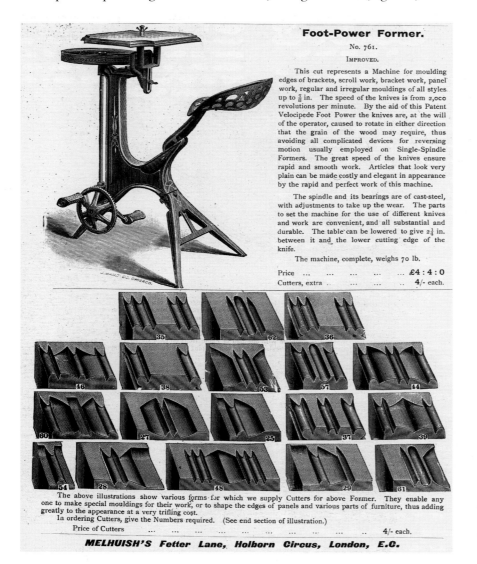

Figure 4
Moulding machine from 1890 catalogue. R. Meluish, Sons and Co., Holborn Circus, London, Tools, machine and hardware merchants. Woodworking machines developed from the late eighteenth century to halve the cost of joinery by the mid-nineteenth century. The development of specialized machines especially between 1870 and 1900 allowed access by ordinary householders to ornate joinery which imitated expensive hand techniques for the insides and outsides of houses, though hand work continued to play an important part in joinery manufacture.

Figure 5
Machines for making bricks were introduced from the 1830s. Clayton and Co's second-sized horizontal brick machine, shown here in a picture published 1868, which combined the crushing rollers, pugmill, and brick-forming in one machine, was employed extensively by large contractors and produce up to 90,000 bricks a week.[13]

Later, the smaller mid-Victorian parsonages of William Butterfield, George Street and Philip Webb, inspired by Pugin's own house, St Marie's Grange, Alderbury, near Salisbury, 1835–6, led to houses such as those in Norham Manor Estate in Oxford of the 1860s.

Suburbs all over the England and Wales reflected early Victorian stylistic variety, houses divided along broadly Gothic or Classic lines, inspired by the eighteenth-century challenge to the idea of Classical authority, and the aesthetic of the Picturesque and Sublime. In north London, houses of the 1830s and 1840s include those shown in Figures 7–10.

Figure 6 Park Village, East, consisting of 'detached houses of various forms with shrubbery in front, and bounded by a low or dwarf wall', from 1823, from C.F. Partington's *Views of London*, 1834, vol 2.

Figure 7
Tudor and Neoclassical style houses on Clifton Hill, St John's Wood, c.1840.

Figure 8
One of several Rural Italianate houses with towers in Little Venice, early 1840s.

The High Victorian eclecticism of the 1860s was characterized by influences from the Continent expanding the range of styles, a new conscious free use and mixing of styles (which had roots in the 1830s), and a growing concern[16] about the direction of architectural style generally. Charles Gray, Charles Hambridge and George Truefitt (Figure 11) exemplify the eclectic approach to house style in London in the 1860s.[17]

Much housing, however, was built in a classical style; top architects did not tend to get involved in the small- to medium-sized housebuilding scene[18] and builders may have preferred to use a style they were familiar with rather than risk building in a fashionable style such as Gothic, which might be hard to sell.

Figure 9
Tudor/Jacobean designs in De Beauvoir Square, Hackney, c.1834–8, by Charles and Hugh Roumieu Gough. Nearby Lonsdale Square (1838–45) also has houses built in the Tudor style by R.H. Carpenter. (Courtesy of Judy Cligman.)

Figure 10
Semi-detached houses in Albion Square, 1846–9, by writer J.C. Loudon, according to Nikolaus Pevsner show the transition from late classical to the Italianate style.[15] Their semi-detached form helped set a pattern which was widely copied. (Courtesy of Judy Cligman.)

Figure 11
George Truefitt's Villa Careno, Tufnell Park, 1865, a 'compromise between Tudor-Gothic and Italian', according to Blackie (see later).

Figure 12
Large Italianate semi-detached villas, Belsize Park Gardens, c.1870–85.

Figure 13
Houses in Osbourne Road, Stroud Green, 1870s and 1880s.

Figure 14
Queen Anne style houses, Muswell Hill.

Figure 15
Arts and Crafts style houses, Muswell Hill.

The 1870s and beyond sees the move towards the Queen Anne and Arts and Crafts styles, in reaction to eclecticism and the diminishing size of country houses. Architects like R.N. Shaw adopted a smaller scale Old English vernacular style, and became involved in the designing of small Queen Anne style houses as models for suburban housing at Bedford Park, London. Builders rapidly adopted the Queen Anne style and also the Arts and Crafts look that followed in the 1890s, as is evident in Muswell Hill, London, where the big builders of the area followed fashion, moving from Queen Anne for houses in the 1890s to Arts and Crafts by 1904[19] (Figures 14 and 15).

A similar stylistic path could be seen in the suburbs of many Victorian towns and cities. For example, Alderley Edge, Manchester had villas of the 1850s built in the Rural Italian style, and even a Swiss villa, Gothic villas of the 1860s and Queen Anne houses of the 1870s and 1880s. Torquay suburbs have many villas in the Rural Italian style, with some Elizabethan and Georgian examples. The Park, Nottingham, begun by P.F. Robinson in the 1820s and completed by T. Hine in the 1850s onwards, shows the move from Georgian terraces and cottage ornés to Rural Italian, Gothic and French Renaissance combinations (Figures 16–18).

Figure 16
Cottage, Park Valley, Nottingham by P.F. Robinson.

Figure 17
Castle Grove, Nottingham by Thomas Hine 1856.

Cardiff, built up from the 1850s, has Robinson-style Tudor cottages, Rural Italian villas, and Queen Anne houses but the predominant style used is Gothic Revival, influenced by Burges, architect at Cardiff Castle and nearby Castell Coch (Figure 19).

The uses of publications ranged from ideas and advice for the middle classes, to essential reading for those involved in building, regarding building legislation, construction techniques and price guidance. Some builders might pay an architect or his assistant for 'a plan or two', but many designed for themselves, and at the lower end of the market especially, there was often no architect involved and so pattern books would have come in useful, to add to the builders' own experience. Advice, designs and so on, where taken from books, was not always the most up to date information available, as builders would have continued to use their old books, for example Nicholson. This helps explain conservatism in design, particularly at the lower end of the housebuilding market, with Georgian being used into the 1880s.[20] Books were certainly intended to be used, either to inspire or to be copied, and often advertised tried-and-tested built designs. Builders could add instant architectural effect with a detail, such as an Italianate campanile, a Gothic doorway, a Tudor, Elizabethan or Dutch gable, a French-style roof, all of which features could be taken from a pattern book and adapted to suit the circumstances. As S.H. Brookes remarked in the preface of his book, *Designs for Villa and Cottage Architecture,* in 1839:

'The efforts of architects in all ages have hitherto been generally directed to public buildings, and to the mansions of noblemen; and those who may be considered as composing the middling orders of society have been for the most part left to become their own architects. Hence the tardiness with which the improvements made in the accommodation, arrangement, and exterior beauty of the mansions of the wealthy have found their way to the dwellings of the middling classes. It is therefore one of the chief objects of the present work, to point out by appropriate designs, how the residence of the man of wealth, and the dwellings of a more humble grade, may in a degree, be equalised as far as regards essential comfort, convenience and beauty. A series of published designs cannot but

Figure 18
Lenton Road, Nottingham, late 1850s.

Figure 19
Late Victorian Gothic Revival houses, Park Place, Cardiff.

prove of great benefit, not only to the experienced, but also to the amateur architect … In rural architecture, particularly, the only means of accomplishing that end, is the study of published designs, for no local builder can be supposed to have had either leisure or opportunity to inspect the different improvements which have gradually or immediately taken place in his own country, or which may be the result of foreign talent. Without recourse to a book of designs, the builder must in his own plans be necessarily tame and uniform, his edifices will but be a copy of each other'.[21]

Names and professions of subscribers in the case of early books, and details of ownership of individual copies give an insight into readership. If proof of the importance of publications were needed, in some cases there are very precise details about the impact of books, as in the case of Robert Kerr's Bearwood, designed for John Walter, the owner of *The Times*, who switched architects and employed Kerr, upon reading Kerr's book.[22] Builders, architects, tradesmen and the public liked to have, and found useful, the various sorts of written material that were published for the different audiences, as is clear from the number and long-running nature of many publications.

THE PUBLISHING WORLD

The role of publications in the production of houses between 1837 and 1901 was not surprising, given that the Victorian period was 'the age of books'.[23] W.J. Loftie in *A Plea for Art in the Home*, 1876, one of Macmillan's 'Art at Home' series of books, spoke of their added ornamental value, 'next to pictures, I am inclined to place books … a well-filled bookcase [is] one of the best ornaments of any sitting-room'. He even recommended certain periods of bindings to suit the style of interior decoration, thus,

> 'There is also a very fine old English style, much sought after, and harmonising very well with Queen Anne furniture and decorations'.[24]

American writer, Julia McNair Wright, whose popular book, *The Complete Home*, 1879, has an entire chapter devoted to 'The Literature of the Home', said 'A Home without books is like a garden without flowers, like a forest without birds or sunshine, like a house without furniture'.[25]

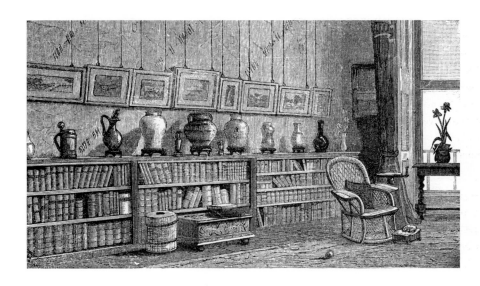

Figure 20
Plate from W.J. Loftie's *A Plea for Art in the House*, 1876.

Reading was a growing activity in the early eighteenth century, evidenced by middle-class magazines, such as *The Gentleman's Magazine,* begun in 1733 by Edward Cave, which was selling 15,000 a month in the 1740s.[26] Reading and writing became an essential ingredient for employment opportunities among the upper working and lower middle classes by the nineteenth century. The 1870 Education Act, which made elementary education compulsory for all, was a further boost to literacy, producing a new generation of adult readers who coincided with the publishing boom of the 1890s; 'many a child has a library that would have sufficed a hundred years ago for a country town', Loftie said in 1876.[27]

The rates of publication for all books rose from approximately 100 new titles a year in 1750, to 600 in 1825, 4400 in 1885, and 6000 in 1899.[28] New trends appeared, with novels overtaking religious subjects as the largest group of new books between 1870 and 1886, and books on trade and economics trebling in the same period.[29] Cheap series emerged, for example, Cassell's 'National Library' of 209 volumes at 3d each in the late 1880s. Magazines also greatly expanded in numbers and circulation; even in 1842, Nathanial Whittock said, 'Persons unaquainted with the Bookselling business can form no idea of the immense sale of the periodicals, particularly the low priced publications'.[30] By the end of the nineteenth century, Harmsworth's *Daily Mail*, begun 1896, costing 1/2d, had a circulation of a million.[31] The use of certain words as selling points in titles of books about the house alters over the Victorian period; for example, 'villa', 'household', 'hints', and 'economy', are replaced by 'house', 'cottage' or 'home', 'taste', 'art', 'artistic', and 'decoration'.

The communications revolution was made possible by technological developments between the mid-eighteenth century and the late Victorian years: steam power, mechanized typecasting and setting, machine-made paper, which reduced the cost of paper in a book from 20% in 1740 to 7% in 1910,[32] and improved means of distribution. Blackie & Son, Glasgow, for example, enlarged their premises 20 times between 1831 and 1874, and introduced machines in the 1830s, and a lithographic department in 1866. Cheaper means of binding came with the invention of the cloth binding in 1823, pioneered by the Clerkenwell bookbinder, Archibald Leighton, and in 1832 gold-blocking motifs on cloth by machine, mainly on the spine of the book, was made possible. Charles Booth said in 1895:

> 'The great reductions in the price of paper and other materials used in the production of books, and the numerous inventions that have facilitated this production, have greatly increased the output and brought books within the reach of all classes just when, by the spread of education, there has begun to be a general demand for them. The movement towards cheapness has compelled the binder to seek by all means to reduce the cost of binding also, and in this he has succeeded, for a book that would have cost 2s to cover ten years ago can now be done for 9d, but the work is not so good, and the increase of such work is turning the mechanic more and more into a machine-minder'.[33]

By 1895 bookbinding was subdivided into 21 distinct trades, for example, book-edge gilder, and marbler. The cost of illustrations, the most expensive aspect of an architectural book in the eighteenth century, were also much reduced under the impact of new techniques which will be discussed separately later.

Architectural books in the eighteenth century were published by one of a number of specialist publishers, such as A. & H. Webly or R. Sayer, or by the author himself, in which case he had to raise capital, execute his own engravings, negotiate with a printer and sell books from home. For example, Thomas Sheraton's *The Cabinet Dictionary* of 1803 was:

> 'Printed by W. Smith, Bookseller, King Street, Seven Dials, and sold by W. Row, Bookseller, Great Marlborough Street; Mathews, No.18, Strand; Vernor and Hood, Poultry; M. Jones, No. 1, Paternoster Row, and by the Author, 8, Broad Street, Golden Square, London'.

A normal print run for architectural books at this time was under 250; William Chambers' *Treatise on Civil Architecture* sold 336 copies.[34] Subscription was a means of selling books, though it was generally not liked;[35] a subscription list gives a flavour of a book, with fewer aristocrats and more craftsmen, the lower the class of book. Selling books in parts or numbers, which began with J Moxon *Mechanick Exercises*, 1678–80,[36] was a popular alternative. The 'Number Trade', as it was known, though much criticized by publishers of whole books, was in 1842 a popular and growing trend, as 'by this means thousands of volumes of an important description have been purchased by a class of readers that would otherwise never have had an opportunity of reading them at all'.[37] By this point, publishing was increasingly diversified, with publishing distinct from bookselling, and periodical publishers, numbers publishers and publishers of whole books established as separate groups.

Along with Rudolph Ackermann of The Strand, I. & J. Taylor of The Architectural Library in Holborn was the major publisher on architecture in the early nineteenth century. Taylor's 1772 catalogue has 14 building titles, rising

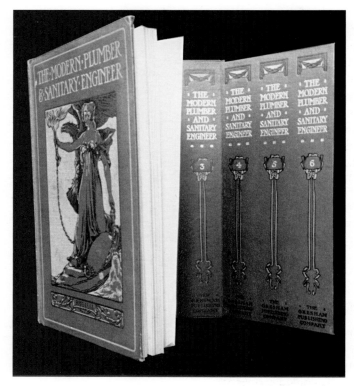

Figure 21
Gresham Publishing Co. Ltd's specimen sample, for demonstration of a set of *The Modern Plumber and Sanitary Engineer*, at 6s per volume.

to 250 titles by the 1818 catalogue. They published the first builder's price book, books by William Pain, and reflected a growing architectural profession,[38] and dominated in this area until Priestley and Weale set up business in the 1820s. As books for the building trades expanded beyond carpentry and building of the eighteenth century to encompass a wide range of trades in the Victorian period, Weale was at the forefront, publishing engineering and building books, alongside works such as A.W.N. Pugin's *True Principles of Pointed or Christian Architecture*, 1841, which sold 1200 copies.[39] John Weale's stock and best-selling Technical Series was taken over by Crosby Lockwood on Weale's death in 1862.

Other established publishers operated in the field of manuals and pattern books (see later) for example, Rivington published Bartholomew's *Specifications*, and later, with Sampson Low, books for Mrs Panton and Mrs Haweis. Longmans published books by J.C. Loudon, Joseph Gwilt, Charles Eastlake and later on, Parker and Unwin, whilst Spon, Kelly and Atchley focused on technical and price books, publishing books by Hood, Nicholson and Brookes. Crosby Lockwood, Hagger and Day & Son, published some expensive pattern books, and books on architectural detail. The early bulk of business for Blackie & Son, publishers of pattern books *Villa Architecture* and *Cabinet Maker's Assistant*, was in the Numbers Trade, at a time when bookshops were rare, except in larger towns, and thus readers were dependent on Numbers, sold by means of travelling, canvassing and delivering.[40] The firm went back to its roots in 1898 when Blackie's formed Gresham Publishing Co Ltd for selling by subscription (Figure 21). Mrs Humphreys six-volumed *Book of the Home* 1909 was sold in this way by Gresham Publishing Co Ltd.

Batsford, established in 1843, developed a speciality in the design field, and its 1863 catalogue had architecture, ornament and fine arts in prime position on the title page. Publishers of Hellyer's *Plumber and Sanitary Houses*, among other books, a unique bond was established between Batsford and writer on ornament, Lewis F. Day, which lasted over 30 years; Day designed the front-papers and endpapers of his books with their initials LFD and BTB interlinked.[41] John Cassell,[42] was the publisher of many books on household related subjects, for example *Cassell's Household Guide*, 1869–71, eventually for a mass market. After working as a carpenter, in a cotton mill and in a velveteen factory, he joined the teetotal movement, and the tea and coffee business in the City of London, and finally began a publishing career with his *Teetotal Times*, followed by many magazines and newspapers set up between 1866 and 1886, including *The Magazine of Art*, 1878–1904. Other publishers of books aimed increasingly at a mass market included Ward Lock who published books for Mrs Beeton. In contrast to the drive towards cheap publications generally, must be set the stands taken to maintain quality in book production by John Ruskin[43] and William Morris' Kelmscott Press.

ILLUSTRATIVE TECHNIQUES IN ARCHITECTURAL AND BUILDING PUBLICATIONS

The general drive towards cutting book production costs also applied to the trend in the use of illustrative techniques in books and journals, so central to the transmission of taste. In the eighteenth century, engraving on copper was the common method used in books for illustrating buildings and their details. Such illustrations tended to be simple outline pictures, which suited the need for precise information about classical detailing. Such a straightforward style of representation also allowed the book to be used as a 'bench book', to work from directly. As Eileen Harris points out, the inconvenience of working from the book when image was necessarily printed separately from text and so one had to turn the page to read the instructions which went with a plate, was solved by authors who put working instructions on the plate itself.

Engraving was, however, a costly process, reflected in the fact that the number of plates in a book was clearly a matter of pride. In fact, it was the most expensive factor in the cost of a book and so many authors undertook their own engravings to keep the costs down. New processes were developed, always aimed at reducing costs rather than improving quality, for example, etching the plate beforehand and then finishing with the burin which became commonplace, and the increasing use of mechanical devices like the pantograph and the ruling machine to the same end. The ruling machine, invented by Wilson Larry in 1790, became greatly used in the nineteenth century especially for backgrounds, skies, borders, etc.[44] Costs were also reduced by the employment of apprentices and young boys to undertake these more mundane tasks. Engraving, later on steel-coated copper, declined in use, but remained the most prestigious form of printed illustration into the Victorian period, the apprenticeship fee averaging £150–250, compared to £50–100 for an aquatint artist or wood engraver in 1842.[45]

Before ruling machines and so on were introduced, tone in engraving had to be created with cross-hatching and stippling. A full range of tone was brought in with the invention of aquatint in the 1760s and was first used in the villa and cottage books of the 1780s and 1790s. It suited the new fashion for the picturesque, adding mood and allowing readers to imagine what their house might look like in a setting. The skill and labour involved in the process gave it a prestigious status. Hand colouring could be added at an extra charge, done by teams of women and children. Between 1785 and 1819, over half all new architectural books included aquatinted plates, particularly in the period from 1800 to 1811 (Figure 23).[46]

Figure 22
Lithographic press, mid 1850s.

Two other techniques came on the scene at roughly the same time which were to eclipse the use of both engraving and aquatint in architectural books, that is, lithography and wood engraving. These media became very important for illustration in the nineteenth century, and lithography was the basis for future developments in the twentieth century.

The importance of wood engraving, first introduced by Bewick in the late eighteenth century, was that type and image were done on the same plate and could therefore appear together on the same page which was much more cost effective than previous techniques. The hard, outline, precise lines suited the need to accurately reproduce architectural detail in the Victorian age of eclecticism. From about 1860, a method of manufacturing wood blocks was developed which involved bolting parts of the block together so different artists could do various parts of the illustration at the same time, useful where time was of the essence, as in the production of a weekly journal, such as *The Builder*.[47] Firms also began to specialize in different types of illustration, for example, in architecture, foliage, machinery, or products for trade catalogues. Commercial considerations of making the process faster and cheaper to meet the huge increase in demand for books and journals led to the use from the 1840s of stereotyping, and electrotyping, which were ways of reproducing the original blocks as casts for the purpose of printing the same image on different machines at the same time (Figure 24).

'The process of engraving is entirely mechanical, that of lithography entirely chemical' (C.J. Hullmandel) (Figure 22).[48] Lithography was available concurrently with wood engraving, though it was eclipsed by wood engraving until later on in the Victorian period. German amateur artist and music publisher, Alois Senefelder, is usually credited with the invention of lithography in 1796. The process was established in Britain by Charles Joseph Hullmandel, and popularized by Rudolph Ackermann who used lithography in his magazine, *Repository of the Arts*. Lithography's ultimate success for architectural illustration

Figure 24
Wood engraving, mid-1850s.

lay in its speed, cheap cost and versatility. As Whittock explained in 1842 'engraving on stone … is cheap, and, when well performed, produces impressions of great beauty in imitation of chalk, mezzotinto, pen and ink, and even of etching … woodcuts, and aqua-tinta. The style, however, which has a decided superiority, is that of chalk, as no copperplate engravings can give so perfect an imitation of original pencil, or crayon drawings'. Its ability in rendering atmospheric picturesque effects led it to appear in nearly half all new architectural books between 1825 and 1831,[49] notably, those of P.F. Robinson and T.F. Hunt, drawn on landscape artist, J.D. Harding, and printed by Hullmandel.

Lithography generally languered behind wood engraving early on though, and had its critics throughout who regarded it as an inferior medium, and not necessarily any cheaper or easier, as T. Hansard put it:

> 'the whole process of drawing on the stone appears, from Mr Hullmandel's treatise, beset with difficulties and dangers of the most teasing and curious description; and is continually liable to failure from, apparently, the most trifling and even ludicrous causes … Even a London winter atmosphere is unfavourable to lithography, as the smoke may fix in greasy particles upon the preparation of the stone, and cause a grey tint to be printed all over the impression'.[50]

However, its potential was clear, and John Ruskin feared for the future of the aquatint artist. In the later decades of the nineteenth century, the tremendous growth in lithographic commercial work called for speedier techniques. Lithographic power-driven machines came in from the 1850s. Pantographs and other forms of reducing and enlarging machines were devised. The lithographic chalk and pen gave way to such inventions as the rub-down shading medium, and the mechanical stippling pen and the aerograph or airbrush. The lithographic trade by then employed large numbers of skilled litho artists, transfer printers, colour-separation draughtsmen and stone preparers.

The process of chromolithography, designed to replace earlier means of colouring books by hand, which was time consuming, costly and ultimately untenable, was first patented by Engelman in 1839. Spurred on by the growing contemporary interest in medieval coloured books, Senefelder, Hullmandel and Baxter also experimented with the technique, as did M. and N. Hanhart, (established in 1830), who produced Pugin's *Floriated Ornament* in 1849, Henry Shaw, who wrote the first of the nineteenth-century books on ornament entitled *The Encyclopaedia of Ornament*, 1842, and Owen Jones, author of *The Grammar of Ornament*, 1856 (still being reprinted in 1910) which had over 100 chromolithographs. Hand colouring continued, using tints like Fielding's and later Windsor and Newton's, sometimes used in combination with printed colour. Full-colour chromolithography was not often used in architecture and building books, which tended to use tinted two- or three-colour tones instead. Trade catalogues and journals also used one-colour lithography, often red or green ink, in the late nineteenth century. Chromolithography was a highly developed craft by the 1860s, using power-driven machines. Mechanical means for producing lines, dots and other patterns, which could be used by lithographic draughtsmen to get tonal effects quickly, were developed in the 1880s by Benjamin Day in the USA. Varnishing by machine also contributed hugely to the look of the late nineteenth-century chromolithograph. Such techniques led to ubiquitous printed matter of all kinds, for example, the trade catalogue (Figure 25), which so epitomized the look of the late nineteenth century, although arbiters of taste often disapproved;

speaking of modern books, Loftie concluded, 'the best have woodcuts, the worst have chromolithographs'.[51]

By 1860, most of the traditional techniques had been developed to their maximum efficiency.[52] In the climate of invention and the more complex needs of trade and society generally, new inventions constantly affected established ways of doing things. In particular the impact of the relationship between photography and printing on publishing was huge. From 1858, wood engravers could engrave from a photographic image, applied by exposing the negative to a light-sensitive coating on the block, which became common practice for magazines and trade catalogues for the rest of the century. Working from photographs in this way gave illustrations of buildings a sense of real perspective, which,

Figure 25
Young and Marten Ltd's designs for stained glass.

combined with the paring down of the use of landscape background as the picturesque fell from fashion, gave Victorian illustrations of buildings an altogether different flavour. Photolithography took over from wood engraving in building journals, such as *The Builder*[53] around 1880. Further experiments with photography led to the development of the halftone screen, invented by Frederick Ives in the early 1880s. It was responsible for the mass-produced photograph, which, along with step-and-repeat machines, changed the face and quantities available of books, catalogues and journals at the end of the century. With such change came further division of labour – artist printmakers, and printing technicians with the aim of cheapening and accelerating the mass production of commercial picture printing. Charles Booth's *Life and Labour of London*, 1895, lists 41 trades under printers, including layeron, taker-of, chromolithographer, lithographic artist, stippler, stone grainer, and photolithographer.

By 1901 the whole range of modern graphic reproduction processes had been developed and were available for use in architectural and building publications. The significance of these developments for ways of illustrating houses were enormous, as will become apparent later in the book.

The following chapters explore publication types in more detail, beginning with eighteenth-century pattern books, treatises, books on the orders, measuring and price books as models from which later publications developed. The mid-nineteenth-century architectural pattern book can be divided into two main types: those by an individual author of all or mainly his own designs, and a smaller group of compilations by leading architectural publishers. By the middle of the century also there was a widening of its scope, to include instructions and advice and, as such, some of these books aimed at a more popular market. Practical books at a range of prices on specific aspects of building, and manuals aimed at householders targetted the growing demand for small- and medium-sized houses and interest in using decoration on the insides and outsides of these houses. Pattern books of house designs continued throughout the period in one form or another, but seemed to decline in numbers as dedicated architectural and building magazines and trade catalogues competed to become the main sources of information and ideas for the house-building industry.

REFERENCES

1 John Archer, *The Literature of British Domestic Architecture 1715–1842*, The MIT Press, Cambridge, Mass. and London, 1985, 274.

2 Stefan Muthesius, *The English Terraced House*, Yale University Press, New Haven and London, 1982, 17.

3 Stefan Muthesius, *The English Terraced House*, Yale University Press, New Haven and London, 1982, 20.

4 T. R. Gourvish, and Alan O'Day, *Later Victorian Britain 1867–1900*, Macmillan, Basingstoke, 1990, 20.

5 Stefan Muthesius, *The English Terraced House*, Yale University Press, New Haven and London, 1982, 27.

6 Christopher G. Powell, *An Economic History of the British Building Industry 1815–1979*, Methuen, London and New York, 1982, 32.

7 James Thorne, *Handbook to the Environs of London*, 1876, reprinted Adams and Bart, Bath, 1970, 697.

8 John Summerson, *The Unromantic Castle*, Thames and Hudson, London, 1990, 232.

9 *Artisans Centenery 1867–1967*, The Artisans and General Properties Company Ltd, 1967, 6.

10 C.G. Powell, *An Economic History of the British Building Industry 1815–1979*, Methuen, London and New York, 1982, 31.

11 H.J. Dyos, *Victorian Suburb*, Leicester University Press, 1977, 124.

12 C.G. Powell, *An Economic History of the British Building Industry 1815–1979*, Methuen, London and New York, 1982, 68.

13 E. Dobson, *A Rudimentary Treatise on the Manufacture of Bricks and Tiles*, Virtue, London, 4th edition 1868, 221.

14 See Stefan Muthesius, *The English Terraced House*, Yale University Press, New Haven and London, 1982.

15 Jones, Edward and Christopher Woodward, *A Guide to the Architecture of London*, Van Nostrand Reinhold Company, New York, 1983, 67.

16 J. Mordaunt Crook, *The Dilemma of Style*, John Murray, 1987, chapter 4.

17 John Summerson, *The Unromantic Castle*, Thames and Hudson, London, 1990, 224.

18 John Summerson, *The Unromantic Castle*, Thames and Hudson, London, 1990, 219.

19 Helen C. Long, *The Edwardian House*, Manchester University Press, Manchester, 1993, 81–2.

20 John Summerson, *The Unromantic Castle*, Thames and Hudson, London, 1990, 219.

21 S.H. Brookes, *Designs for Cottage and Villa Architecture*, Kelly, London, 1839, iii.

22 J. Franklin, *The Gentleman's Country House and its Plan, 1835–1914*, Routledge and Kegan Paul, 1981, 122.

23 Asa Briggs, *Victorian Things*, Penguin Books, London, 1990, 217.

24 W.J. Loftie, *A Plea for Art in the Home*, Macmillan, London, 1876, 80.

25 J. McNair Wright, *The Complete Home*, J.C. McCurdy, Philadelphia, 1879, 216.

26 P. Langford, *A Polite and Commercial People: England 1727–1783*, Oxford University Press, Oxford,1992, 91.

27 W.J. Loftie, *A Plea for Art in the Home*, Macmillan, London, 1876, 75.

28 R. Ensor, *England 1870–1914*, Oxford University Press, Oxford, 1992, 328.

29 R. Ensor, *England 1870–1914*, Oxford University Press, Oxford, 1992, 159.

30 N. Whittock, *The Complete Book of Trades*, 1842, 41.

31 Asa Briggs, *Victorian Things*, Penguin Books, London, 1990, 306.

32 *Encyclopaedia Britannica*, Chicago, 1970, 467.

33 C. Booth, *Life and Labour of the People in London*, Macmillan, London 1903 edition, second series, 2, 233–59.

34 John Archer, *The Literature of British Domestic Architecture 1715–1842*, The MIT Press, Cambridge, Mass. and London, 1985, 8.

35 Eileen Harris, *British Architectural Books and Writers 1556–1785*, Cambridge University Press, 1990, 55.

36 Eileen Harris, *British Architectural Books and Writers 1556–1785*, Cambridge University Press, 1990, 56.

37 N. Whittock, *The Complete Book of Trades*, 1842, 40.

38 Eileen Harris, *British Architectural Books and Writers 1556–1785*, Cambridge University Press, 1990, 59.

39 P. Atterbury and C. Wainwright, eds, *Pugin A Gothic Passion*, Yale University Press and V&A, 1994, 157.

40 Blackie, Agnes A.C., *Blackie and Son 1809–1959*, Blackie & Son Limited, London and Glasgow, 5 .

41 See Hector Bolitho, *A Batsford Century*, 1943.

42 See Simon Nowell Smith, *The House of Cassell 1848–1958*, 1958.

43 A.F. Mumby and I. Norrie, *Publishing and Bookselling*, Jonathan Cape, London, 1974 edition, 272.

44 Gavin Bridson and Geoffrey Wakeman, *Printmaking and Picture Printing*, The Plough Press, Oxford and The Bookpress Ltd, Williamsburg, Virginia, 1984, 87.

45 N. Whittock, *The Complete Book of Trades*, 1842, 491.

46 John Archer, *The Literature of British Domestic Architecture 1715–1842*, The MIT Press, Cambridge, Mass. and London, 1985, 31.

47 Ruth Richardson and Robert Thorne, *The Builder Illustrations Index 1843–1883*, The Builder Group and Hutton and Rostron, in association with Institute of Historical Research, University of London, 1994, 20.

48 T.C.Hansard, *Typographia: An Historical Sketch of the Origin and Progress of the Art of Printing*, Baldwin, Craddock and Joy, 1825, 889.

49 John Archer, *The Literature of British Domestic Architecture 1715–1842*, The MIT Press, Cambridge, Mass. and London, 1985, 32.

50 T.C. Hansard, *Typographia: An Historical Sketch of the Origin and Progress of the Art of Printing*, Baldwin, Craddock and Joy, 1825, 898.

51 W.J. Loftie, *A Plea for Art in the Home*, Macmillan, London, 1876, 73.

52 Gavin Bridson and Geoffrey Wakeman, *Printmaking and Picture Printing*, The Plough Press, Oxford and The Bookpress Ltd, Williamsburg, Virginia, 1984, 16.

53 Ruth Richardson and Robert Thorne, *The Builder Illustrations Index 1843–1883*, The Builder Group and Hutton and Rostron, in association with Institute of Historical Research, University of London, 1994, 33.

2 Architectural pattern books and manuals for Victorian houses

EARLY MODELS

Eighteenth-century building activity inspired a flurry of books, including new types introduced to cater for specific needs. Books available on building and decoration included architectural treatises, notably Isaac Ware's *A Complete Body of Architecture*, 1756–7 and William Chambers' *Treatise on Civil Architecture*, 1759, much reprinted, with additions by other authors, for example Joseph Gwilt, through to 1862. There were two types of pattern book,[1] firstly those by well-known architects of their executed designs, such as James Gibbs' *Book of Architecture*, 1728 (see Figure 26).

The second, much larger group of pattern books, written by building craftsmen or architects, contained untried, ideal patterns, sometimes copied from other books. Such books were intended to be used, for example, in rural areas instead of using an architect, and their designs were indeed widely copied. Two popular

Figure 26
Plate from Robert Adam's *Works in Architecture*, 1773. (Courtesy of the Trustees of Sir John Soane's Museum.)

and influential writers in this field were Batty Langley and William Halfpenny, who each wrote about 20 books related to architecture and building. William Halfpenny's books, including *New and Compleat System*, 1749, which gave suggestions for cheap houses, *Chinese and Gothick Architecture, Properly Ornamented*, 1752, and *Twelve Beautiful designs for Farmhouses*, 1750, spread Palladian and rococo motifs all over the country. His first book, *Practical Architecture*, 1724, which was reissued over the next 40 years, was an early book on the orders, to be of practical use in providing workmen with a system for calculating proportions, as 'this is a great Labour and Hindrance to those who are well acquainted with Arithmetick, and to those who are not ready and expert at it' (Figure 27). The first major treatise on the orders followed, namely, James Gibbs' *Rules for Drawing the Five Orders*, 1732.[2]

Pattern books were often portable books for the practical use of the builder, for example Batty Langley's *The Builder's Jewel*, 1741, and its many subsequent editions to 1808. Langley's practical approach is clear in *The City and Country Builders and Workman's Treasury of Designs*, 1740, published through to 1770, thus:

> 'The study of architecture is really delightful in all its process; its practice is evidently of the greatest importance to artificers in general; and its rules so easy, as to be acquired at leisure Times, when the Business of Days is over, by way of diversion.'

Its 400 engraved designs for gates, doors, windows, chimney pieces, pavements, bookcases, ceilings, and ironwork provided a wide choice for builders and aided customers in conveying their preferences to the workman (Figure 28). Such designs followed fashion but showed craftsmen how to adapt classical orders and ornamental parts to any building or piece of furniture. Langley's patterns were widely copied in London and elsewhere,[3] and undermined regional variety in architecture.

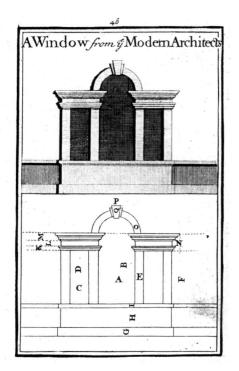

Figure 27
Plate from Halfpenny's pocket-sized *Practical Architecture*. Calculations were on each left-hand page.

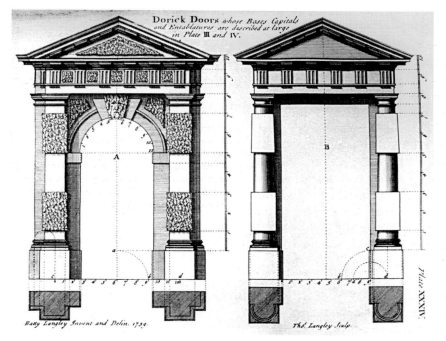

Figure 28
Plate from Langley's *Treasury of Designs*. (Courtesy of Architectural Resource Centre, Cardiff University.)

Aside from designs for carpenters in pattern books such as those mentioned, the first manual to cover geometry and construction thoroughly was Francis Price's, *The British Carpenter, or a Treatise on Carpentry*, 1733, sixth edition 1768.[4] His book led to further carpentry manuals from the 1750s by Abraham Swan and William Pain, whose popular works were also reproduced in the USA. Pain's *The Practical House Carpenter*, 1789 revised by S.H. Brooks in 1860–1, and published by Weale, was typical of the way Georgian manuals were re-used in the Victorian period. Pain's *The British Palladio; or Builder's General Assistant*, 1786, was more of a pattern book than a manual, consisting of plans, elevations and sections, designs for doors, chimneypieces and ceilings 'with their proper embellishments in the most modern taste'; his books made accessible and popularized the 'Adam style'. Above all, the book aimed to be of practical use, stating in the preface the aim to demonstrate:

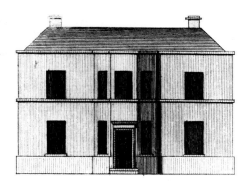

> 'in the most easy and practical method, all the principal rules of architecture, from the grand plan to the ornamental finish … this work will be universally useful to all carpenters bricklayers, masons, joiners, plasterers and others … their proper ornaments for practice drawn up to half size to which are added scales for enlarging or lessening at pleasure.'

A practical pattern book of house designs, well used in the USA and in Britain, was John Crunden's *Convenient and Ornamental Architecture, Consisting of Original Designs for Plans, Elevations and Sections Beginning with the Farm House and Regularly Ascending to the Most Grand Villa Calculated for Both Town and Country and Suitable to Persons in Every Station of Life*, 1767, with seven further editions to 1815 and still in use in the nineteenth century. Crunden, a landscape gardener, architect, surveyor, and manufacturer of artificial stone, aimed his book at the middle classes; among the 222 subscribers there were 52 subscribers connected with the arts of building and decoration, only eight peers, and no architects.[5] It contained measurements and explanatory notes, along with designs which ranged from plain designs 'where elegance is not required', to grander Palladian schemes (Figure 29).

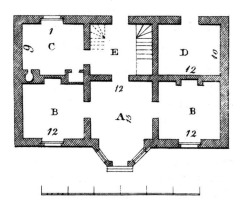

A new type of book of house designs for the middle classes emerged in the later eighteenth century. Containing minimal text and designs set in aquatinted landscaped backgrounds, allowing readers to imagine what a house could look like, the so-called villa and cottage books were essentially aspirational books and popularized leading ideas of the day such as those of Sir Humphrey Repton. The first villa book, and also the first architectural book to use aquatint as a means of illustration, was *Rural Architecture and Design or Designs from the Simple Cottage to the Decorated Villa*,[6] published in 1785 by architect and surveyor, John Plaw, who went on to write two further books. It comprised 62 aquatinted plates of views and plans and a brief list of the plates. The designs included cottages and various sizes of villa, mainly in the classical style, each in a picturesque landscaped setting (Figure 30).

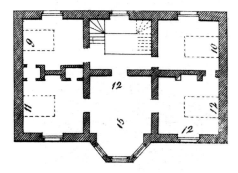

Figure 29
An elevation for a small house, to be built near town for the use of a tradesman. It consisted of A vestibule, BB parlours, C Kitchen, E staircase, one pair of stairs, and a floor containing a dressing room and four bed chambers. (Courtesy of the Trustees of Sir John Soane's Museum.)

Many of the designs in Plaw's book were built and clients named, and the book was clearly a means of advertising his work to readers. There were 215 subscribers to the 1790 edition, which cost £2 2s, included ten peers, four baronets, seven MPs, six clergymen, ten military officers, 32 surveyors, 16 architects, 15 bricklayers, eight builders, eight carpenters, seven painters, three members of the Royal Academy, two engravers, two masons, a landscape draughtsman, a plasterer, a bookseller, an alderman, a surgeon, and two comedians.[7] *Rural Architecture* was very popular, reaching its sixth edition by 1804.

This book was followed by many books along similar lines over the next few decades, including those by James Malton, Charles Middleton, Edward Gyfford, T.D.W. Dearn, Richard Elsam, and W.F. Pocock. James Malton, a pioneer of picturesque rural cottage orné, was central to a keen debate about the cottage in the early nineteenth century. His ideas were expounded in books such as *An Essay on British Cottage Architecture; Being an Attempt to Perpetuate on Principle, that Peculiar Mode of Building, which was Originally the Effect of Chance*, 1798, where he urged readers 'to take the cottage under protection; which, unless speedily done, will be found to exist nowhere but on the canvas of the painter'; Richard Elsam responded in *An Essay on Rural Architecture, Being an Attempt, Also to Refute the Principle of Mr James Malton's Essay on British Cottage Architecture*, 1803. A number of villa books were written by young architects, for example, W.F. Pocock's *Architectural Designs for Rustic Cottages, Picturesque Dwellings, Villas, etc. With Appropriate Scenery*, 1807, Joseph Michael Gandy's forward-looking *The Rural Architect,* and *Designs for Cottages, Cottage Farms and Other Rural Buildings*, both 1805, and David Laing, *Hints for Dwellings* 1800 (Figure 31).

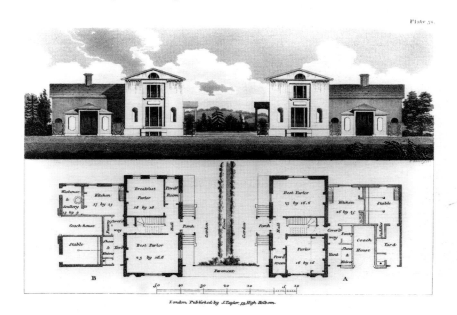

An important villa book from the early nineteenth century was J.B. Papworth's *Rural Residences, Consisting of a Series of Designs for Cottages, Small Villas and Other Buildings with Observations on Landscape Gardening*, published in 1818, second edition 1832; it was compiled, after 'having received such applications for the series of designs in a separated form' from his designs first published in Ackermann's *Repository of the Arts* in 1816–17. Papworth was a founder member of Government Schools of Design, the Institute of British Architects, and RIBA vice-president, also landscape gardener, and prolific designer of housing schemes, conservatories, glassware and furniture.

Rural Residences, illustrated with hand-coloured aquatint plates, consisted of labourers' cottages, cottage ornés and villas, and ornamental buildings, and ranged from a villa for an artist, or man of literary study, in a Rural Italianate style, to designs for an ice house, a Gothic conservatory, garden seats and a verandah for a London dwelling (Figure 32). Each design was accompanied by several pages of text on style, purpose and practical building details. Papworth comments on the lack of the architect's presence in contemporary building practice thus:

> 'the villas that surround London, the country residences of the most wealthy of its inhabitants not being designed by the architect, are little more than cases of brick, in which a certain number of apartments are injudiciously arranged, presenting to the eye a continuity of ill-bestowed expense and tasteless absurdities … in London also the speculative builder has generally superseded the labours of the artist, for the architect is rarely called upon … the modern streets of London present repetitions of the same vapid elevations of mere perforated walls'.

The purpose of the book was instead, ' to attempt to instill into the public mind a real love for architecture, by developing its principles and practice'.

Figure 32
Design for a park entrance in Papworth's *Rural Residences*.

ARCHITECTURAL PATTERN BOOKS AND MANUALS 1820–50

This period of time, as has been suggested, saw stylistic variety in house design, in reaction to the long period of domination of the Classical style. Architectural pattern books were a major vehicle for transmitting ideas about style to the public and architectural professions. The pattern book continued throughout the early Victorian period, and the variety of forms it took widened with new printing and illustration techniques and expanding markets for books. In this period we see pattern books of a single architect's designs, compilations of various named designers' work, pattern books of untried designs, or a combination of untried and built, the combination pattern book/manual/encyclopaedia, and books on correct historical architectural detailing.

Villa and cottage books thrived in the 1820s and 1830s, for example, *Villa Architecture, A Collection of Views with Plans of Buildings, Executed in England, Scotland*, etc. 1828, reprinted 1855, the last of three books by Robert Lugar. Lugar was widely known as a designer of cottage ornés and Nash-style castellated Gothic mansions. It followed the standard format with a short introduction, 42 hand-coloured aquatints and etchings of built designs in Birmingham, Liverpool and elsewhere, in a wide range of styles and sizes including Gothic houses, an Indian villa and a Turkish summer house (Figure 33). Like other pattern book writers, Lugar was designing for new wealthy industrialists; this book is dedicated to William Crawshay, owner of the Cyfarthfa ironworks of Merthyr Tydfil, which by the 1840s was the world's largest iron-producing company. The book illustrates Cyfarthfa Castle, built in 1824 high in the hills overlooking the works; Lugar's castellated style, with its chunky, coarse detailing and loose planning, according to Henry-Russell Hitchcock looks forward to the Victorian period. It cost £30,000 to build which drew criticisms from Crawshay's father: 'Is it wise to build on so large a scale? No man can say what it will cost to finish, furnish and maintain'. But Crawshay boasted that Cyfarthfa Castle eclipsed all other residences in Merthyr 'a thousand times', with a 'lake larger than 50 fish-pools', vast hot houses, 'and an ingenious ice-house for keeping game and meat in perfect condition'.[8]

Figure 33
Small dwelling for William Currie, near Guildford, designed by Robert Lugar. (Courtesy of Cyfarthfa Castle Museum and Art Gallery.)

As mentioned in the Introduction, one of the most important pattern book authors was Peter Frederick Robinson, a founder member of Institute of British Architects and one of its first vice-presidents. A prolific designer of cottages and villas, his main contribution to the debate about style in the early nineteenth century was through his pattern books. He introduced the Swiss chalet, and in particular, his Old English/Tudor designs were copied or adapted by builders and architects over the following decades. Indeed the influence of the Tudor style ran through to the Vernacular revival and Arts and Crafts styles of the late nineteenth century, and beyond to twentieth century interwar housing. The first of Robinson's six books, *Rural Architecture; or, a Series of Designs for Ornamental Cottages*, 1823 (Figure 34), published in 12 parts, was, according to John Archer, the first collection of designs in the 'Old English' style, which, Robinson stated in the preface:

'has been of late years altogether neglected. The high pointed Gable, and enriched chimney stack; the ornamental barge board, and mullioned window; the ivy-mantled porch, and lean-to roof, have given place to the spruce square built house and tiled roof, assuming the fashion of our modern tradesmen's

Figure 34
Frontispiece to P.F. Robinson's *Designs for Ornamental Cottages*, 1836 edition.

villas, with sashed windows and central door, formality even extending to the outbuildings. The great change which features of this class have produced within the last twenty years is the subject of much regret … With a view to restore a style peculiar perhaps to this country, these designs are now presented to the Public; many of them have been erected and the attempt has been to unite economy with elegance'.

Sales of the book proved 'very extensive', and it ran to a fifth edition in 1850, with the 1836 edition stating that 'as many of the plates were newly worn out, they have been redrawn at considerable expense'. Robinson's books were, as mentioned earlier, remarkable also for their lithographs printed by Hullmandel, the medium's constant improvement alluded to in the 1836 edition, thus, 'the art of lithography has considerably improved since the publication of the original work'. Each design in the book was represented by several illustrations, pen and ink-style lithographs of front and side elevations, plans, and scenic view in chalk-style lithography, often drawn by Harding (Figure 35).

Figure 35
Cottage in the Old English style by P.F. Robinson.

Robinson's *Designs for Ornamental Villas,* 1827, fourth edition 1853, contained the largest range of styles to be so far published by 1827, with 16 designs in the Swiss, Greek, Castellated, Elizabethan, Palladian, Norman, Tuscan styles; exotic styles were omitted as not being appropriate for the British climate (Figures 36–38). The Swiss chalet was introduced to Robinson on travels on the Continent in 1816, and much imitated by most subsequent pattern book

Figure 36
Villa in the Tudor style in Robinson's *Designs for Ornamental Villas,* 1838 edition.

Figure 37
Anglo-Norman villa.

Figure 38
Library of a Grecian villa.

DESIGN. N.º 2.

Figure 39
A gate lodge at Singleton, South Wales, in a Swiss style for H. Vivian, an important copper manufacturer.

writers of the 1840s. Vivian was an important client (Figure 39); Robinson's other books also show designs for him, a bailiff's cottage and a seaside villa Oystermouth, and even a whole book devoted to the design of Vivian's Singleton Hall, entitled *Domestic Architecture in the Tudor Style,* 1837. Other titles by Robinson included *Designs for Farm Buildings,* 1830, with designs in the Old English, Italian, Swiss and Rustic styles 'to show the humbler shed may be erected with some regard to effect'. *Village Architecture, Being a Series of Designs ... Illustrative of the Observations Contained in the Essay on the Picturesque by Sir Uvedale Price,* 1830, fourth edition 1837, with its picturesque view of a street of houses of contrasting styles, inspired Joseph Paxton and John Robertson's houses at Edensor in Derbyshire, 'a perfect compendium of all the prettiest styles of cottage architecture from the sturdy Norman to the sprightly Italian', according to *The Gardeners' Chronicle* in 1842.

Designing along similar lines to Robinson was Thomas Frederick Hunt who wrote the first detailed study of Tudor architecture, entitled *Exemplers of Tudor Architecture, Adapted to Modern Habitations,* 1830, reprinted 1841. In contrast to Robinson's highly picturesque effects, Hunt depicted his Old English houses and their settings very differently in his books, *Half a Dozen Hints, or Picturesque Domestic Architecture in a Series of Designs for Gate Lodges, Gamekeeper's Cottages, and Other Rural Residences,* 1825, and other editions to 1841, and in its sequel, *Designs for Parsonages, Houses, Alms Houses, etc., With Examples of Gables, and Other Curious Remains of Old English Architecture*, 1827. Hunt declared in the preface of *Designs for Parsonages* that there would be:

'no factitious effect obtained by the broken, unequal, or painter's line; the individual forms are represented with the sharpness of recent finishing; and the small portions of vegetation which appear on some of the roofs are only such as a few months would produce.'

He added, 'a small portion of ornamental work, tastefully disposed is capable of producing very considerable effect' (Figure 40).

A key source for the Rural Italian vernacular style, so popular with housebuilders all over Britain, was Charles Parker's *Villa Rustica,* published in 16 monthly parts, from 1832 to 1841, second edition 1848; it followed Hunt's *Architettura Campestre* of 1827, and occasional designs in the style included

Figure 40
A parish clerk's house and grave digger's hut, from *Designs for Parsonages,* which also included a curate's house, clergyman's house, vicarage, rectory, almshouses, and four parsonages. (Courtesy of Architectural Resource Centre, Cardiff University.)

in even earlier books such as Papworth's *Rural Residences*. Parker's book, based on sketches of buildings done in Italy, had 93 lithographed plates of actual buildings, their plans and details, from around Rome and Florence (Figure 41). His book's usefulness to housebuilders lay in showing how the Italian style could be adapted for use in Britain:

> 'Throughout the whole country, and especially near Rome and Florence, there exist a great number of habitations … The peculiar object therefore of the work will be to delineate the exterior of these buildings, with their surrounding scenery, modifying the interior to the wants and manners of this country. Although on the Continent collections have been made and published … they are generally confined to palaces, and pass by or omit the humbler class of dwelling.'

Of the three types of villas in ancient Roman times – Urbana, Rustica, and Fructuaria – Parker chose Villa Rustica as his model.[9]

Features such as the tower, 'its peculiar form is so identified with Italian scenery, that without it we scarcely recognise the landscape as complete', and the low, projecting roof, proved very popular as they were easily copied by villa builders and lent instant style to even a small house. At the top end of the scale, Thomas Cubitt owned a copy of Parker's book and it perhaps influenced the design of Osborne House (Figure 42).

Figure 41
A farmhouse on the Florence to Prato road. Parker estimated that it would cost £450 to build in Britain. The plans show the ground floor with a central kitchen, and scullery and dairy. The upper floors had large parlour and small bedroom, with two bedrooms above. (Courtesy of V & A Picture Library.)

OSBORNE.

Figure 42
Osborne House, Prince Albert and Thomas Cubitt, 1845–51. Note, there was also a Swiss chalet built in the grounds for the Royal children in 1853.

On the question of architectural style that was such a central debate of the time, at this point many pattern book writers appear to have been happy to be able to provide clients with a wide range of ready-made options to choose from, as originality was not thought necessary and yet it was felt that a general set of rules could not be applied in all situations.[10]

There was however an increasing interest in historical accuracy in style. One of the principle figures in this respect and a keen supporter of the Elizabethan style was Henry Shaw, who published *Details of Elizabethan Architecture*, 1834–9, sold in parts, 5s each, with many plates drawn and engraved by himself. It was a book mainly about details of external and internal ornament from houses such as Blickling Hall, Norfolk, with some interiors of rooms, 'a subject rarely entered into' (Figures 43 and 44). The intention was:

> 'by a selection of some of the more interesting specimens of architectural detail, the true source is pointed out from which information may be derived … a collection of genuine examples must prove a useful guide in making a restoration of an ancient edifice, where it is absolutely necessary to follow out the minutest details with care and accuracy.'

The book was important in establishing and popularizing the Elizabethan style as an alternative to the Neoclassical style; 'Elizabethan architecture has established well-founded claims to public notice, and it is no longer necessary to apologize for a zealous attachment to the pursuit of its characteristic features … the style, with all its exuberance and variety of detail, has been adopted with success in the designs of several considerable mansions recently erected', such as Harlaxton, Lincolnshire, which displayed 'correct adherence to propriety of design'.[11]

Gothic was given its theoretical underpinning most fervently by A.W.N. Pugin. His father, A.C. Pugin, was responsible for establishing historical accuracy in the Gothic style, and his book, *A Series of Ornamental Timber Gables from Existing Examples in England and France of the Sixteenth Century*, 1831, was very influential among domestic architects of the day. Augustus Welby Northmore Pugin pressed for adherence to the Early English and Decorated Gothic as a national style, arguing in *True Principles of Pointed or Christian*

Figure 43
A portion of the painted frieze in the dining room at Gilling Castle from Henry Shaw's book.

Figure 44
'Ancient' leadwork.

Figure 45
Pugin's *Details of Antient Timber Houses*. (Courtesy of Architectural Resource Centre, Cardiff University.)

Architecture, 1841, that Swiss cottages were only suitable in Switzerland and Renaissance architecture in Italy. It was in his principles, such as truth and honesty of construction, that his influence ultimately lay. He effected this influence in part through his commitment to cheap, mass-produced publications aimed at a mass audience, specifically students and middle-class enthusiasts, by the use of cloth bindings and embossed designs. In his books such as *Gothic Furniture in the Style of the Fifteenth Cent. designed and etched by A.W.N Pugin*, 1835, *Details of Antient Timber Houses*, 1837 (Figure 45), and *Contrasts*, 1836, his use of cloth bindings, with the title page stuck on the front in lieu of expensive gold blocking, meant he could sell such books at 12s each, compared to Henry Shaw's *Specimens of Ancient Furniture* which cost two guineas.[12]

A new interest in suburban housing appeared in books at this time. Very much a working book of designs, *Original Designs for Cottages and Villas, in the Grecian, Gothic and Italian Styles of Architecture*, came out in 1831, written by Edward William Trendall, a London architect. With its plain lithographed outline illustrations of houses in the classical style, it was a pattern book aimed at instructing builders rather than impressing clients, and, most importantly, was the first book dedicated to smaller house designs for the growing suburban environs of large cities and towns. Books by Plaw and Laing, already mentioned, had hitherto included occasional designs, but the subject had not been focused on until now. J.C. Loudon's manual/pattern book, *The Suburban Gardener and Villa Companion*, 1838, second edition 1850, which gave examples of gardens for the four rates of house, the fourth type being the typical garden of a small suburban house, first used the term 'suburban' in the title of a book.[13] Costing 20s, The *Journal of Agriculture* called it 'The most complete work on villa gardening that has ever appeared in our language' (Figure 46).[14]

John Claudius Loudon stands out as a prolific writer of magazines and books on architecture and gardens. His most well-known book, *Encyclopaedia of Cottage, Farm and Villa Architecture*, 1833, costing £3 3s, was a landmark in nineteenth-century architectural and building publications; containing over 2000 wood engravings, and spread over more than 1000 pages, the book incorporated patterns for house types from villas to farms and cottages, in the by now standard range of fashionable styles to suit all tastes, including Grecian, Tudor, Swiss and Italian (Figures 47–49). The *Encyclopaedia* was more than just a pattern book of architectural exterior styles and plans. It was a complete guide to house and garden style, with practical advice on the decoration, fitting up, and furnishing of the interior as well as the exterior treatment. It incorporated contributions from 50 specialists, E.B. Lamb, Charles Parker, P.F. Robinson, T.F. Hunt and T.J. Ricauti and sold 'at such an unprecedentedly low price, as must insure, to the names and talents of our contributors, an extensive circulation'. Loudon popularized the contents of books, aimed at 'men of wealth', rather than builders or amateurs, for example, , by reproducing their work in his books.

The actual production of the book was a huge effort, with never more than four hours sleep and 'drinking strong coffee to keep ourselves awake'.[15] It made use of the potential of wood engraving, reproducing text and pictures together which gave a completely different format and appearance from other books

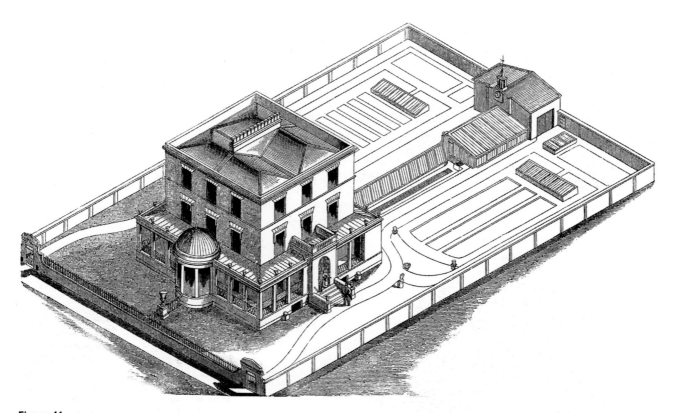

Figure 46
Loudon's own house in Porchester Terrace, Bayswater, 1837–8, was dealt with in detail in *The Suburban Gardener and Villa Companion* and popularized the semi-detached house and garden ideal.

on the market at the same time. It helped him to meet his aim of producing his book as cheaply as possible, as part of his wider aims to bring good design to a mass audience and argue for art and design as a standard part of the education curriculum. Loudon's *Encyclopaedia* was extremely popular as a pattern book for builders and the public alike, running to 14 editions or impressions over the next 40 years, and is arguably one of the most influential publications on design in the nineteenth century, *The Times* declaring 'No single work has ever effected so much good'.[16] It was very successful in North America also, where it influenced A.J. Downing in his books, such as *The Architecture of Country Houses,* 1850. Much of its mass appeal was due to its practical, instructive approach, emphasizing fitness, convenience and comfort and domestic ideals of the time. This approach was vital in the formation of attitudes to design in the Victorian period, and in his ideas on the beauty of truth, he was following a similar path to Pugin,while at the same time accepting eclecticism in design.

Alongside those authors, such as Pugin, Shaw and Parker, who championed particular styles, the pattern book of designs where all styles were portrayed without bias to meet the builder's needs, or client's personal preferences, continued to be produced. Francis Goodwin's *Domestic Architecture, a series of designs in the Grecian, Italian and Old English Styles*, 1833–4, £2 12s, is a typical example. Goodwin had a large architectural practice in the Midlands and was ready to build in any style, though was known better for Gothic designs (Figures 50–51).

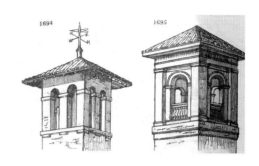

Figure 47
Left: Italianate watch-tower, common on small villas in Tuscany. Right: campanile, 'calculated to produce an excellent effect' in J.C. Loudon's *Encyclopaedia of Cottage, Farm and Villa Architecture.*

LXI.

LXII.

Figure 48
Designs in London. Plate LXI is a dwelling with three rooms on the ground floor and a back kitchen. Of this design, Loudon says, 'There is something mean and depressed about the elevation of this building; though to some tastes. this would be a recommendation to it, as a cottage'. Plate LXII is a design for a house with four rooms on two floors. Loudon remarks that, 'On the supposition that this house is to be seen principally in front, we consider it handsome', but concludes generally it is 'unexceptionable'.

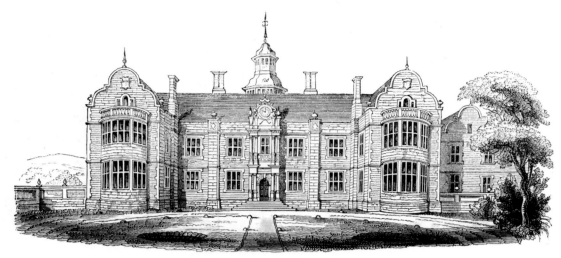

Fig. 1436 is the entrance front, as seen from within the gate of the entrance court.

Figure 49
Loudon's chose the Elizabethan style for his 'beau ideal of an English villa'.

Figure 50
Francis Goodwin's Gate Lodge for Henry Horden, Staffordshire, £250, accidently set on fire by workmen before it was completed. (Courtesy of Architectural Resource Centre, Cardiff University.)

OU   OV   OW   OX

OY   OZ   PA   PB

PC

PD   PE

YOUNG & MARTEN, LTD. STRATFORD, LONDON, E.

PRICES OF THESE DESIGNS ARE GIVEN ON PAGE 54

MUSIC

DESIGNED IN YOUNG & MARTEN'S, LTD. STAINED GLASS STUDIOS.

Lenton Road, Nottingham, late 1850s (Figure 18).

Design for a park entrance in Papworth's *Rural Residences* (Figure 32).

Small dwelling for William Currie, near Guildford by Robert Lugar (Figure 33). (Cyfarthfa Castle Museum and Art Gallery)

Previous page: Young and Marten Ltd's designs for stained glass (Figure 25).

A portion of the painted frieze in the dining room at Gilling Castle from Henry Shaw's book (Figure 43).

Frontispiece from Pugin's *Details of Antient Timber Houses* (Figure 45). (Architecture Resource Centre, Cardiff University)

Francis Goodwin's Gate Lodge for Henry Horden, Staffordshire, £250, accidently set on fire by workmen before it was completed (Figure 50).

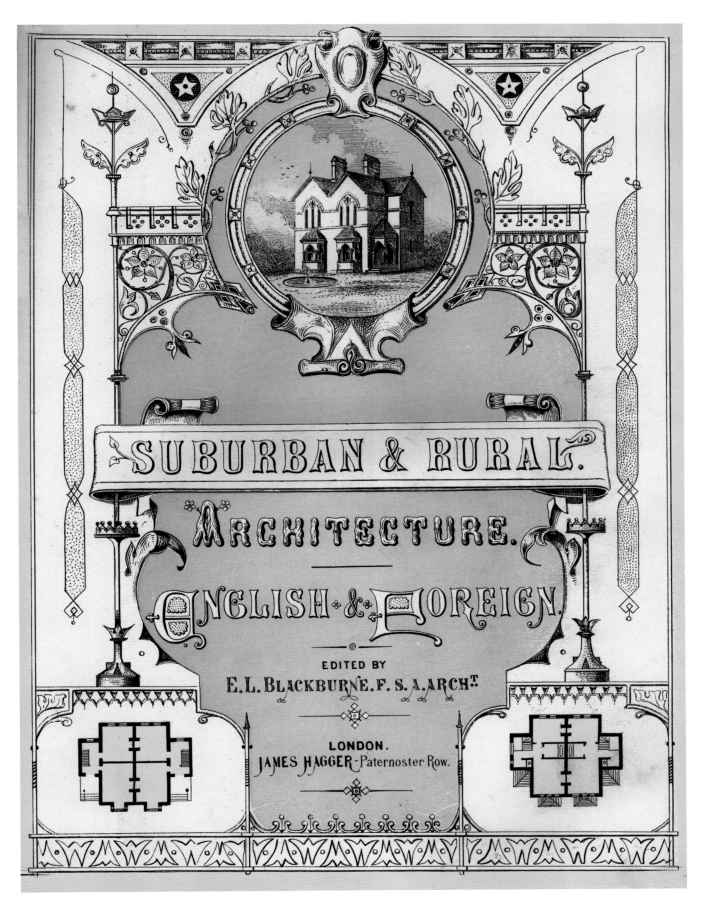

Title page to Blackburn's book (Figure 69).

A French Gothic detached villa (Figure 70).

DETAILS OF PORCH.

C.

A.   ELEVATION.   SECTION.   B.

Detail of an Italian lodge (Figure 72).

Figure 51
A Grecian villa in Goodwin's book, the most expensive design at £4930 for a brick and stucco front with stone cornices and plinths (stone ashlar front cost £936 extra). (Courtesy of the Trustees of Sir John Soane's Museum.)

Reissued as *Rural Architecture* in 1835, and with a supplement, as *Cottage Architecture*, also 1835, this work was popular and was still being reprinted in 1850. It drew some criticisms, however, in Loudon's *Architectural Magazine*, in 1834, thus,

> 'In some published designs for villas, Parker's, for example, the fascination of the landscape prevents a critical examination of the building; and the general character and keeping are such as would render any structure pleasing. There is no danger of this kind, however, to be apprehended from the landscapes in Mr. Goodwin's book; these, in almost every case, detract from the effect of the building, rather than add to it. What are more especially offensive in our eyes are the trees, many of which are like nothing in the vegetable kingdom; … in Plate 35, there is a tree, the form of which sets at defiance even the uncouth shapes of the trees of Australia'.[17]

As already noted, the first book devoted mainly to terraced houses, *Builders' Portfolio of Street Architecture*, came out in 1837. Its author was J. Collis, District Surveyor for Lee, Charlton and Kidbrooke for 46 years. The subject of the terraced house had cropped up only as isolated examples in books prior to this, and had generally been relegated to price books and some builders' manuals. It was similar to Trendall's book in its practical outline drawings, and contained 19 Neoclassical designs for facades of houses and other buildings (Figures 52 and 53).

Figure 52
Title page to J. Collis' *Builders Portfolio of Street Architecture*. (Courtesy of Nancy Sheiry Glaister.)

The growth of the suburban villa, already highlighted by writers such as Loudon, was also acknowledged in S.H. Brookes' *Designs for Villa and Cottage Architecture*, 1839:

> 'An Englishmen when he first travels on the Continent … particularly remarks … on the comparatively small number of suburban villas which are seen in the vicinity of even the largest towns, and which form such a delightful feature in the landscape scenery of England. … Par eminence, England becomes the country of suburban villas.'

Brookes' book was a pattern book for builders and clients, full of details on construction to help builders, as well as the usual array of styles – Swiss, Gothic, Elizabethan, classical – for villas and cottages, apparently largely unexecuted. But Brookes is an author who signals a change in feel towards later years.[18] The

Figure 53
First-rate house by Collis. (Courtesy of Nancy Sheiry Glaister.)

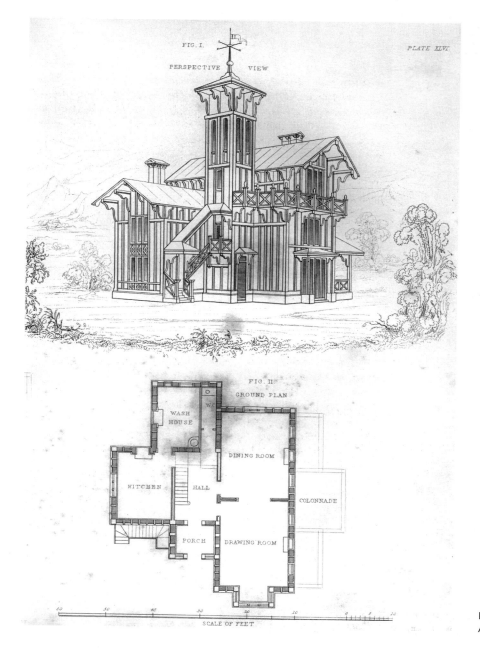

Figure 54
A Swiss design by Brookes.

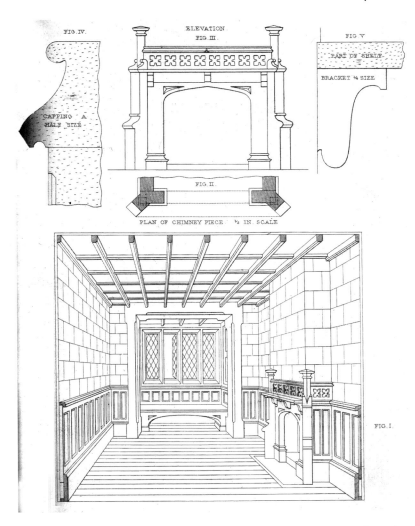

Figure 55
A Gothic interior scheme by Brookes.

style of depiction is different from Goodwin or Robinson; gone is the coloured aquatint or chalk-style picturesque lithograph, to be replaced by simple, outline steel engraving and hard, machine ruled lines, strong perspective and minimal scenery and the forms are Victorian in feel (Figures 54 and 55). Brookes also always wrote for technical publishers such as Kelly and Atchley and his books have a 'down-to-earth' flavour about them. As an author whose books were published until the end of the Victorian period, his books reflected the changing priorities towards catering for the small builder, and new modes of depicting buildings.

Nineteenth-century stylistic variety reached new heights in the 1840s with the 27 designs in Richard Brown's *Domestic Architecture, Containing a History of the Science and Principles of Designing Public Edifices, Private Dwelling Houses, Country Mansions and Suburban Villas, With Dissertations on Every Branch of Building, From Choice of Site to Completion of the Appendages*, 1842. Travels on the Continent in the 1820s (as with many other writers mentioned) inspired the largest number of styles to date, including a Venetian summer residence, a Flemish-style chateau, a Chinese casino, and other dwellings in the Florentine, Swiss, Egyptian, Grecian, Roman, Persian, Morisco-Spanish, and Plantagenet styles. That such designs were in demand is shown by the publication of a second edition in 1852, but it was not so much the more exotic total designs which would have been copied but rather, their details (Figure 56).[19] The book covered

Figure 56
Norman, Tudor, Grecian and Roman residences in their appropriate situation and scenery. This plate from Richard Brown's book was accompanied by a few pages of advice on 'choice of situation, as well as that of the design of the residence … of paramount importance'. (Courtesy of V & A Picture Library.)

architectural theory and practice as well as style, along with landscape gardening, and as such was more than simply a villa pattern book or practical manual.

Books by John Ruskin, 'a man to whom England owes measureless gratitude in matters of art',[20] which proved seminal for High Victorian Gothic, came out in the late 1840s and early 1850s. His ideas contained in *The Seven Lamps of Architecture*, 1849 (see back cover), and *The Stones of Venice, 1851–3,* on smooth flush surface decoration, tracery, different coloured materials, truth, repetition of forms, massiveness, and so on were inspired by Italian medieval architecture. This filtered through to housebuilding in the form of polychrome decoration, created by bands of contrasting coloured brick or stone, now economically possible following the repeal of the Brick Tax in 1850, which became widely used on house fronts until the end of the century. The bay window, approved of by Ruskin, was also a ubiquitous feature of mid to late Victorian houses.

THE 1850S AND 1860S

Pattern books of the 1850s and 1860s were varied, some were books of patterns for villas along conventional villa book lines, while others appealed more directly to builders. There was also a new emphasis on house planning which led to publications addressing this aspect of the house. The way houses were depicted became more straightforward, discarding landscape views and concentrating on details of style and layout. Much more information was given on specifications, prices, specific brands of product, and so on. Chromolithography was used in architectural pattern books in this period for the first time, and those using colour by Tarbuck and Blackburne (see below), were published by Hagger of London, but printed in Leipzig and Dresden by A.H. Payne who had set up there in the 1830s. Pattern books focused on the middle-class villa, and many now included designs for small terraced and semi-detached houses as well. Interest in the cottage had by now shifted to one which was more philanthropic, under pressure from industrialization, from early books like John Hall's for the Society for Improving the Condition of the Working Classes, to those of Henry Roberts in the 1860s (Figure 57) and John Birch in the 1870s.

A good example of very much a working pattern book/manual of instruction primarily for builders is Edward Lance Tarbuck (editor), *The Builder's Practical Director, or Buildings for all Classes, Enabling Every Freeholder to be His Own Surveyor and Builder: Containing Plans, Sections and Elevations for the Erection of Cottages, Villas, Farm Buildings, Dispensaries, Public Schools etc. With Detailed Estimates, Quantities, Prices etc.*, 1855–8. It is a roughly assembled compilation of articles on details of construction, site, drainage, and building law, alternating with a range of plans and elevations by Tarbuck, S.H. Brookes and Gardiner and Son, many of which were combination block and hand coloured, and clearly done by different hands. With the numerous building societies being set up at the time, and the Freehold movement of the 1840s and 1850s, Tarbuck's intention was 'to lay before our readers a Handbook of Building, a reference to which will be of use to the initiated as well as those

Figure 57
Labourers' cottages in John Vincent's *Country Cottages*, 1860.

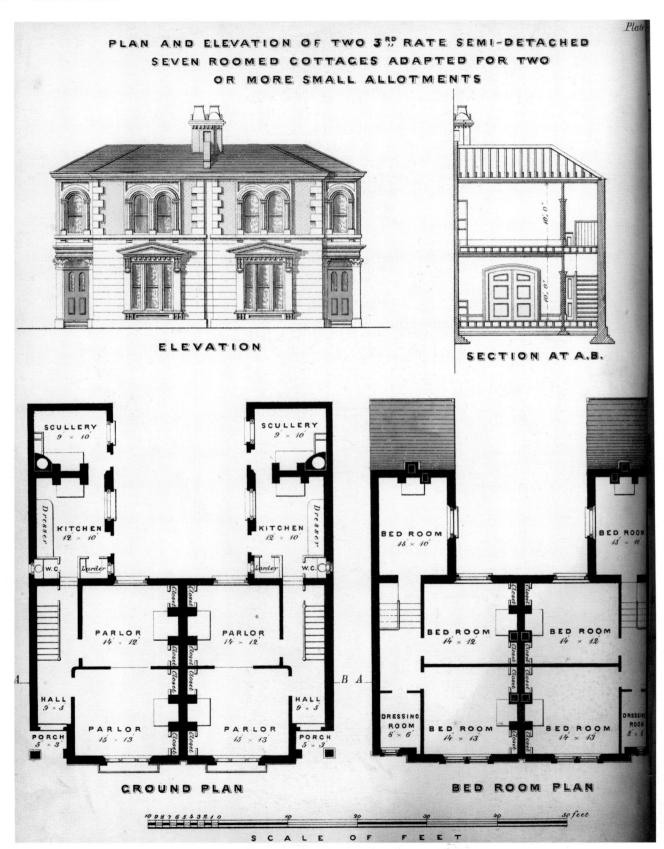

PLAN AND ELEVATION OF TWO 3ᴿᴰ RATE SEMI-DETACHED
SEVEN ROOMED COTTAGES ADAPTED FOR TWO
OR MORE SMALL ALLOTMENTS

ELEVATION

SECTION AT A.B.

GROUND PLAN

BED ROOM PLAN

SCALE OF FEET

Figure 58
Design for third-rate houses costing £560 a pair to build in *The Builder's Practical Director*.

about to purchase plots of ground or to build houses'. Designs ranged across all sizes of house 'from the cottage of the labourer to the residence of the Esquire', but what is significant are the designs for small suburban houses (Figures 58 and 59). Designs, presented without comment on styles other than labels attached, were generally Italianate of some sort, with a few Gothic, Elizabethan for detached dwellings, with even a pair of castellated Gothic semi-detached villas. An architect and surveyor, Tarbuck clearly wrote for the practical man, writing also *An Encyclopaedia of Practical Carpentry and Joinery*, 1857–9, *Handbook of House Property* 1875, fifth edition 1892, and contributing regularly to *The Builder* and *Building News*.

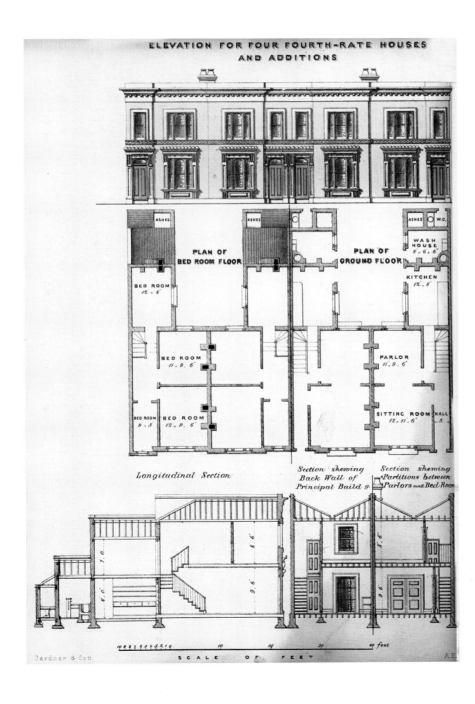

Figure 59
Fourth-rate houses costing £750 to build in total.

ELEVATION.

ONE PAIR.

GROUND PLAN.

Figure 60
House in St John's Wood from Weale's book. (Courtesy of Architectural Resource Centre, Cardiff University.)

PADDINGTON ESTATE.
2ND CLASS.

ELEVATION.

GROUND PLAN.   ONE PAIR PLAN.

Figure 61
Houses in Paddington. (Courtesy of Architectural Resource Centre, Cardiff University.)

Weale's compilation of 1857, *Designs and Examples of Cottages, Villas and Country Houses, Being the Studies of Several Eminent Architects and Builders*, was even more disjointed, comprising designs ranging over a 50-year period; early nineteenth-century villa book aquatints of detached country houses by C.A. Busby, architect of Kemp Town and Brunswick Town, Brighton, and Edmund Aiken, sit alongside contemporary simple outline illustrations of designs by Thomas Tatlock and others for suburban villas and terraces built

TORIANO AVENUE, KENTISH TOWN.
SMALL 3RD CLASS.

ELEVATION. 39 FT. 6 IN.

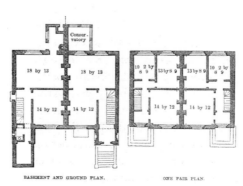

BASEMENT AND GROUND PLAN.   ONE PAIR PLAN.

COST £500 THE PAIR.

Figure 62
Kentish Town housing. (Courtesy of Architectural Resource Centre, Cardiff University.)

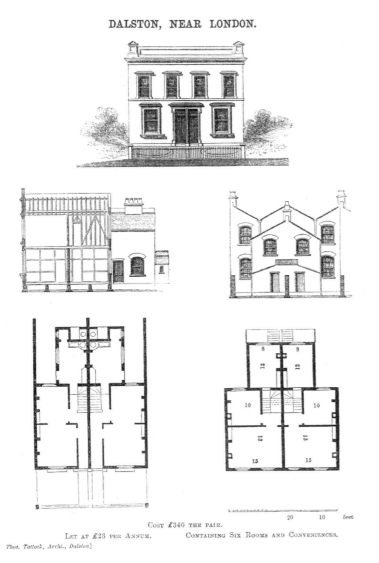

DALSTON, NEAR LONDON.

COST £340 THE PAIR.

LET AT £28 PER ANNUM.   CONTAINING SIX ROOMS AND CONVENIENCES.

Thos. Tatlock, Archt., Dalston]

20   10   feet

Figure 63
Houses in Dalston. (Courtesy of Architectural Resource Centre, Cardiff University.)

in London and the south-east of England (Figures 60–63). Like Tarbuck's book, the majority of designs in Weale's book were in an Italianate style, with a few Gothic designs. A compilation from sources so diverse in time, type of dwelling and method of depiction, suggests the basic conservatism of the housebuilding industry in that such a range would be considered relevant to building needs.

Typical of the mid 1850s is *Designs for Villas, Parsonages and Other Houses*, by Samuel Hemming. The book has semi-detached and detached house designs, adaptable to the terraced type, costing between £200 and £5000.[21] A narrower and more expensive market was sought by Charles Wickes with his *Handy Book of Villa Architecture*, published in two series from 1859 to 1862. Prices ranged from £1125 for a two reception room, five bedroom and bathroomed, Gothic-style house. The cheaper houses in Wickes' book were in the Old English style, with Italianate, Jacobethan, and polychromatic fashionable French Gothic and renaissance reserved for more elaborate designs (Figures 64–66). It followed the traditional pattern book format, with no introduction except a list of plates, but prices, materials, brands for fittings and their sources were given in very precise detail, and plans, sections and elevations were drawn from every angle, so prospective clients could imagine each house in detail. For example, an Italianate villa costing £2975 with four reception rooms, seven bedrooms and a balcony, had a marble or Minton encaustic tiled floor, along with Bielefeld or Jackson papier mâché decorations to the sum of £80. The emphasis given to new materials and technologies, such as the bathroom, and up-to-date conservatory construction according to Paxton's system, reflects the developments in manufacturing and services by 1862.

Front Elevation.

SCALE OF FEET

Day & Son, Lith.rs to the Queen.

Figure 64
An old English half-timbered design by Wickes costing £1479.

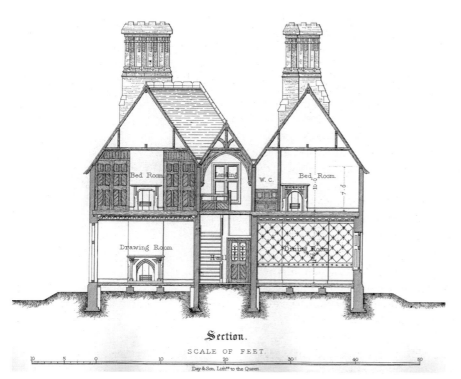

Section.

SCALE OF FEET.

Day & Son, Lith.rs to the Queen.

Figure 65
Section through the design in Figure 64. Detailed sections of the interior with fittings show the increasing attention paid to interior style by the middle classes, instigated in part by the availability of cheaper ready-made and easily assembled decorative components.

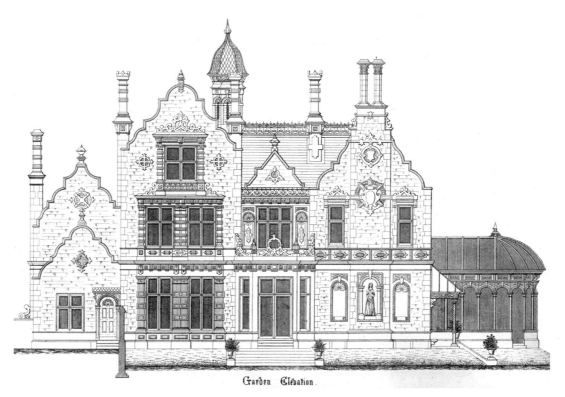

Garden Elevation.

Figure 66
The most expensive design from Wickes' more flamboyant second series, costing £3036.

Published in the same year as Wickes, but catering for other end of the market, was S.H. Brookes' *Rudimentary Treatise on the Erection of Dwelling-houses or the Builder's Comprehensive Director*, specifically aimed at the young builder, for Weale's Technical Series, costing 2s 6d. Basically a manual, rather than a pattern book, it nevertheless gave elevations and plans of a classical-style, semi-detached house, giving the reader an uncomplicated example to follow. It was this straightforward approach which led to this books' enduring popularity (see page 67). There was a flood of books, particularly in the second half of the 1860s, which coincided with the contemporary building boom. Other cheap books included J.W. Bogue's *Domestic Architecture*, 1865, a small practical guide of 38 pages, with designs and costs, with a section on handy hints on internal arrangements, by R.S. Burn. Robert Scott Burn was a prolific writer on a very wide range of subjects from ornamental drawing for students (Figure 67), carpentry, and conservatories, to steam engines and profitable pig keeping between the 1850s and 1890s. His books on architecture and building included *The Grammar of House Planning*, a small 'thoroughly practical' book written in 1864, with ideas taken from the work of A.J. Downing, and *The Builder* and *The Building News*. Costs were kept down using simple line diagrams rather than expensive illustrations. It was a book intended for house investors, house proprietors, men of practice and students of architecture on style and giving 'a wide variety of plans ranging from … the simplest cottage … to the more pretentious country villa and town mansion'. His book aimed to give not just a series of plans but using the same plan, offering alternative arrangements for doors, windows and fireplaces, a need 'much felt in practical literature'. Heating was also dealt with, reflecting the contemporary interest in the services of the house.[22]

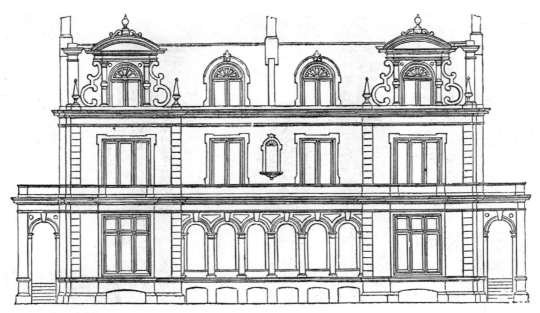

Figure 67
Elizabethan semis from Robert Scott Burn's *Ornamental Drawing and Architectural Design*, a cheap book published by Ward Lock, 1857.

Robert Kerr, originally from Aberdeen, became a founder member and first President of Architectural Association in 1847 at the age of 24, and later, Professor of the Arts of Construction at King's College London. His landmark book, *The English Gentleman's Country House*, 1864, retitled in 1871 as *The Gentleman's House, or, How to Plan English Residences, From the Parsonage to the Palace; with Tables of Accommodation and Cost, and a Series and Selected Plans*, contained 40 lithographed ground plans; many were taken from *The Builder* and *The Building News*, and included several by Kerr himself. Kerr described the history of styles used for the gentleman's house, the nineteenth century 'Opening with that Palladianism which had long been the vernacular of Europe, it introduced very soon the fastidious Greek; became involved more slowly, but even still more surely, in the romantic Gothic; spared a liberal portion of attention for the dainty Elizabethan; and gave still greater attention to the eminently serviceable Non-Palladian Italian; all the while openly avowing more or less the novel but striking doctrine of Eclecticism, that all are equally good in their way'.[23] The plan of the larger house had, Kerr explained, followed a similar path, 'Under the general freedom of thought which prevailed at the commencement of the century … the practice of the Palladian plan was becoming irksome … At the same time there was arising … that singular competition of contrary ideas which, in due course, has ripened into a direct antagonism, in all arts and letters alike, between Classicism and Gothicism of style.' He continued that: 'its present practice is an Eclecticism which adopts the Palladian and other Italian models on the one hand, and the Elizabethan and pure Medieval on the other, quite indiscriminately and interchangeably.' Robert Kerr indicated the eclectic approach to style in his day, 'In what Style of Architecture shall you build your house? A universal question these days, in England if not elsewhere … The architect will generally put this query to his client at the outset of their intercourse; and if the client be inexperienced in such matters, he may be somewhat astonished to discover what it is he is invited to decide upon … he is expected to make a choice from among half-a-dozen prevailing 'styles', all more or less antagonistic to each other, all having their respective adherents and opponents'.

Figure 68
Kerr isolated ten fashionable styles which a client, who was 'the pay master, and must therefore be the pattern-master' could choose from.[24]

Kerr's book also covered rooms of the house, and details such as the bay window. His 12 principles of planning in a gentleman's house, however small were, privacy, comfort, convenience, spaciousness, compactness, light and air, salubrity, aspect and prospect, cheerfulness, elegance, importance, and ornamentation.[25] Chapter titles, such as 'How to employ a builder', 'How to employ an architect', 'How to build inexpensively', 'How to deal with exterior design', show its useful and comprehensive qualities, similar to Loudon's *Encyclopaedia*.

Edward Lushington Blackburne, architect of many churches, and Dioscesan surveyor to Norwich, edited *Suburban and Rural Architecture: English and Foreign*, in 1867, reprinted in 1869 (Figure 69). It contained a selection of designs, some built for houses in a range of styles and was primarily a picture book. Descriptions such as 'Anglo-Italian', 'Italianized Gothic', 'Tudor-Gothic' and 'German' demonstrate well the eclecticism of the day and the inclusion of a wider range of continental influences, led by architects such as William Burges. All the villa designs were coloured using three-colour tint rather than full chromolithography (Figures 70–72). In contrast to the villa

Figure 69
Title page to Blackburne's book.

Figure 70
A French Gothic detached villa.

Figure 71
Swiss semis.

DETAILS OF PORCH.

C.

A.   ELEVATION.   SECTION.   B.

Figure 72
Detail of an Italian lodge.

designs, and more forward-looking, were the uncoloured designs by Shaw and Lockington's designs for cottages and small terraced houses in Portland cement concrete (Figure 73).

Brothers George Ashdown and William James Audsley, well known for their books on ornament, such as *Polychromatic Decoration as Applied to Buildings in the Medieval Style*, 1882, a practical guide for architects and decorators, with 36 chromolithographed plates, published *Cottage Lodge and Villa Architecture*, in 1868. In contrast to Blackburne's range of styles, this book favoured Gothic and related styles. Quoting from Pugin, Ruskin and G.G. Scott, this book outlined the choice between national styles, first revived by Pugin, and 'domestic Italian', arguing that 'It is to be desired that one style of architecture should be adopted by us in the present day; but we cannot hope to see that desirable end attained, so long as individual taste and fancy are allowed to rule in matters of architecture'. The book made the case for Gothic as the most suitable and tractable style, while Elizabethan, either in its half-timbered, or palatial form, though not so beautiful, was also approved of. Even the domestic Italian style, which was 'too well known … to require any description', it was admitted that, 'as a style for villa buildings, it has its advantages' (Figures 74 and 75).

Front Elevation.
Scale 8 feet to an Inch.

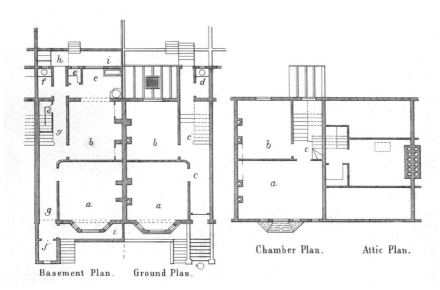

Basement Plan. Ground Plan.

Chamber Plan. Attic Plan.

Figure 73
Small terraced houses; £270 for each house.

Around the same time, Blackie's brought out a large, expensively produced volume, a copy of which was owned by Robert Kerr, entitled *Villa and Cottage Architecture, Select Examples of Country and Suburban Residences Recently Erected*. The book aimed to fill a perceived need for more books of designs for distinct classes of middle-class houses, as opposed to country houses or small, cheap houses, both of which were well provided for. The book was also a response to continual demand for designs by top British architects whose

'alleged indifference to advantages, private and public, that are calculated to accrue from the dissemination of representations and written particulars of executed designs, has been contrasted with the readiness of Continental architects to publish elaborate monographies of their chief productions.'

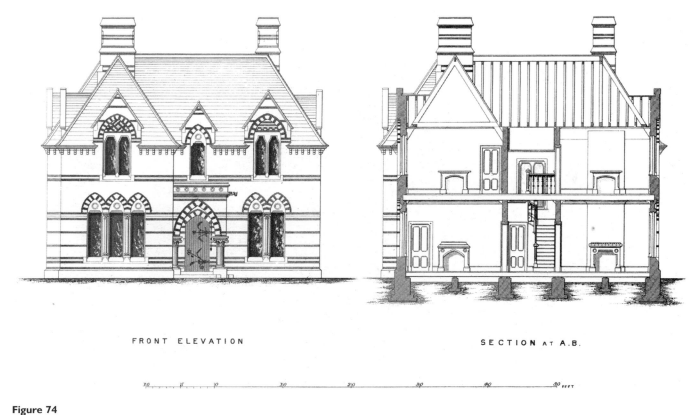

FRONT ELEVATION   SECTION AT A.B.

Figure 74
Gothic design in Audsley, using polychromatic decoration in the form of bands of ornamental brickwork, following Ruskin's advice and examples by William Butterfield. Audsley declared in the preface, 'if we build our houses of one colour of stone, a painfully monotonous effect is certain to be the result'.

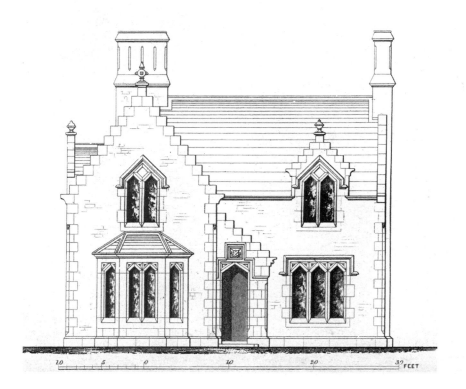

Figure 75
Audsley also recommended Old Scotch, in both baronial and small crow-stepped gable house form, as being flexible and effective. It was said 'As far as towers are concerned, the Old Scotch style gives greater opportunity to the modern designer, more so than perhaps the Gothic itself; and in a villa a well-designed entrance tower or angle turret is a feature which never fails to give value and interest to the composition ... We cannot recommend the adoption of the castellated or battlemented tower, which has been so fashionable of late years'.[26]

Cottage · Orné · – · Mill · Green · Essex

Alternative Design

Figure 76

Henry Kendall's. Cottage orné in the style of the period 'from the fifteenth to seventeenth century', Mill Green, Essex, 1845 in Blackie's book. This design and its alternative version were also used in Turnham Green, Kensington, Childerditch, Aldershot, Twickenham and Cambridge. (Henry Kendall had himself written a pattern book, *Modern Architecture*, issued in three series between about 1846 and 1856. The large format volumes (first series cost £1 11s 6d) each contained 12 hand-coloured lithographed views, roughly half of which were designs by Kendall, of houses in the London area. These included Italianate villas built in Camden, Hampstead, Notting Hill and Regent's Park and houses in Kensington Palace Gardens, including one by Owen Jones.)

Figure 77
Alexander Thomson's, double villa in an adaptation of the Greek style, near Glasgow, 1856–7.

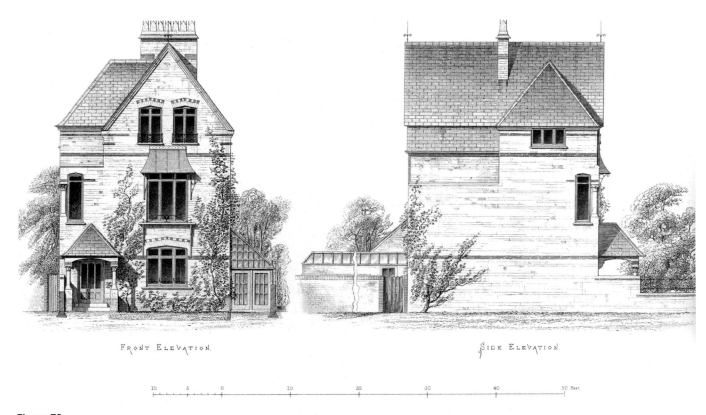

FRONT ELEVATION.   SIDE ELEVATION.

Figure 78
Design by G. Truefitt (pupil of L.N. Cottingham) for a house in Middleton Road, Tufnell Park, London, 1859 in a broadly Gothic style, 'greatly modified and adapted to materials and requirements of the day'.

EAST OR ENTRANCE ELEVATION.

Figure 79
House designed by Banks and Barry for Banks on Sydenham Hill, London, 1862, regarded as particularly successful because 'seldom is the work of an architect produced without interference from his employer'.

Generally dismissing past works as collections of untested designs, with a single plan and pictorial view, or representations historical structures and details, this book went into much greater detail than other pattern books mentioned, showing each design in full and the 'considerable diversity in internal arrangements, in the structural treatment of materials, and in decorative character, or style and ornamental detail'. This book was intended to be a source of inspiration and guide to prevent costs overrunning, rather than a copy book.[27] There were 31 houses 'of moderate dimensions, or erected at a cost ... ranging from £500 to £2500, but including some examples of more expensive character' illustrated, all built in the previous 20 years by 19 different architects including Banks and Barry, Henry Darbishire, David Cousins, Ewan Christian, Speakman and Charlesworth, Edward Walters, and E.B. Lamb. Examples were from London, the Midlands, the North and Scotland (Figures 76–79 and Figure 11).

ARCHITECTURAL BOOKS 1870–1901

Two books came out in 1870 which showed the continuing popularity of the Elizabethan and Jacobean styles. One of these was Thomas Morris, *A House for the Suburbs*, not a book of patterns, but a social and architectural sketch of the suburban house, with the ideal shown in the frontispiece. It was 'a popular subject, treated in a popular style',[28] and covered a wide range of topics from suburban society, to the cost of land, and gave average prices for styles of architecture, thus, an unornamented Italian parsonage at £1100, would cost £1400–1600 if done using rich Gothic detail, and £1700 with Tudor/Elizabethan detailing. Beaumanor Hall, Leicestershire, by his old tutor William Railton, cost £10,000 by comparison.

FIGURE XV. ITALIAN EXTERIOR OF GLEBE HOUSE.

Figure 80
T. Morris gave Italian and English alternatives for the same exterior.

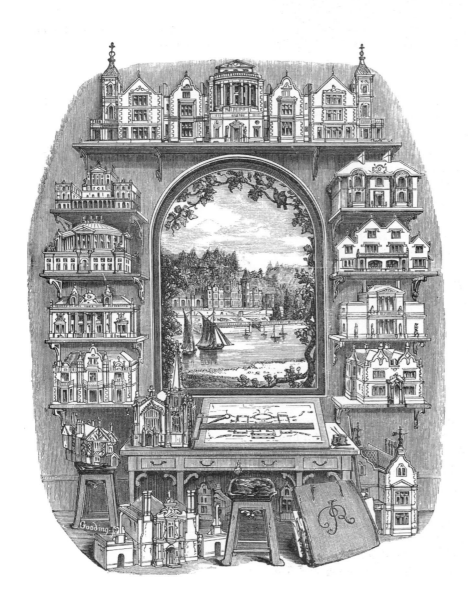

Figure 81
Title page from C.J. Richardson's book.

Figure 82
Vine Cottage, Blaise Hamlet, 1810. (Courtesy of The National Trust.)

A popular book in Britain and in the USA was *Picturesque Designs for Mansions, Villas, Lodges, etc. with Decorations, Internal and External, Suitable to Each Style,* 1870, by C.J. Richardson (Figure 81). A former pupil of Sir John Soane, and one of the evening masters of the Head Government School of Design, Somerset House. *Picturesque Designs* was a less extravagant book than his earlier works, such as *Architectural Remains*, 1837–40, costing £3 5s for colour and gilt illustration. Its 500 wood engravings of dwellings and garden buildings in a range of styles, included one cottage adapted from Vine Cottage at Blaise Hamlet by John Nash (Figures 82–83). The name of the book changed with the second edition in 1871, to a more modern sounding title, *The Englishman's House,* and ran to a fifth edition in 1898, appearing in New York in 1873 as *Housebuilding, From a Cottage to a Mansion.* Other books aimed at a popular market included *A Freehold Villa for Nothing* by I. Marvel, 1871, a small, practical manual aimed at the amateur builder, with advice on repaying loans and how to employ an architect to draw up specifications for £20 and design a front elevation for a guinea (Figure 84).

In the late 1850s and early 1860s, Eden W. Nesfield and Richard Norman Shaw, pupils of Gothic Revivalist, Edmund Street, following Pugin's lead, had published books of sketches of historical architecture done in France, Italy and Germany (Figures 85–87). Shaw and Nesfield rebelled against their Gothic past a few years later, turning instead to sources like Dutch and English seventeenth century domestic architecture for inspiration. The Queen Anne style for town housing, characterized by an eclectic mix of red brick, sash windows, and Dutch gables, was the result. J.J. Stevenson's Red House of 1871 was London's first example of Queen Anne. In country housebuilding, there was a change following the agricultural depression of the 1870s to building smaller, less costly houses.[29] What emerged instead was the Old English style of Nesfield and Shaw, using pargetting and half-timbering. This picturesque cottage style had links back to the cottage style of P.F. Robinson and others; Nesfield and Shaw were also taught by J.D. Harding who did illustrations for Robinson's books.[30] A new

Perspective view.

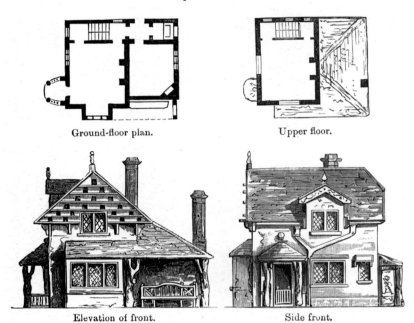

Ground-floor plan.　　　　Upper floor.

Elevation of front.　　　　Side front.

Figure 83
Richardson's version of Vine Cottage.

consensus emerged, in contrast to previous decades, and the designs of lead-ing architects for smaller houses at Bedford Park, for example, were copied and adapted by younger architects and builders (Figures 88 and 89).

The part played by publications, and in particular, by journals, in this trans-mission of the Queen Anne style is also very significant. The numbers of pat-tern books seem to slow in this period but there are some significant books. Shaw, in collaboration with architect-trained W.H. Lascelles, who patented a precast concrete slab system in 1875, published a pattern book of designs, *Sketches for Cottages and Other Buildings Designed to be Constructed in the Patent Cement System of W.H. Lascelles*, 1878 (Figure 90). Lascelles' houses were illus-trated in a popular manual, Shirley Foster Murphy's *Our Homes and How to Keep Them Healthy*, 1883, which had 16 contributors dealing with the topic of healthy houses (Figure 91).

Figure 84
'Italian villa style' semi, costing £340 each house, demonstrated prevalently conservative taste.

Figure 85
Shaw's *Architectural Sketches from the Continent*, 1858, title page.

Figure 86
Timber houses. Shaw hoped the book's 'chief utility may be found in its suggestive tendency. We have recently commenced to draft on our national style many beauties and peculiarities hitherto confined to the continent'.

Figure 87
Nesfield's *Specimens of Medieval Architecture Chiefly Selected from Examples of the 12the and 13the Centuries in France and Italy*, 1862 included Italian Gothic popularized by Ruskin and Street. Only a few of the lithographs are by Nesfield, as he explains, 'I much regret, that, through other pressing duties, I have been prevented from lithographing more than a limited number of plates myself'. The original binding was considered very forward looking; Nesfield says in a note to Captain Crewe Read, dated August 1873 in this copy, 'very sorry that I cannot get one of the original copies – but have tried everywhere'.

Figure 88
House in Bedford Park. (Courtesy of David Long.)

Figure 89
House in Richmond. (Courtesy of David Long.)

Thomas Cutler, Vice President of the Architectural Association, and a well-known designer of small country houses, wrote a pattern book of half-timbered and brick Shaw-style designs in 1886 (Figure 92).

The case for the Queen Anne style was made in *House Architecture* by J.J. Stevenson, published in 1880. Looking at the question again of 'in what style shall we build', and taking each style in turn, the book argued that although Gothic was more flexible for houses than classic and had 'in late years the full tide of enthusiasm, eloquence and fashion in its favour',[32] it was impractical when it came to grates and gasoliers, and the problem of blinds and curtains for pointed windows. He also described the French style, which with its tall roofs was lately very fashionable, as producing a 'good deal of show for the money',[33] and on the Scotch style, commonly used for country houses in the previous 20–30 years, as 'all mustard and no beef'–[34] although he praised the plain style of Scottish house. The average housebuilder had not used Gothic much because according to Stevenson, he did not understand it, and because he 'would not risk building Gothic houses for sale',[35] which Stevenson considered was an astute assessment of the market. Builders had instead continued using debased classical styles, especially Italianate (Figure 93). Stevenson favoured using a style which was 'a true and national style', reflecting the vernacular of workmen, based in the classic styles of the past 300 years, and yet expressing characteristic modern 'accurate mechanical finish'.[36] The best solution to the problem of style was therefore perceived to be the recent fashion for so-called Queen Anne, which was 'a builder's style', which combined cut brick and moulded terracotta, with curved and classic details, and Gothic-inspired flat wall surfaces (Figure 94). Stevenson recommended the style personally to readers in his own house, 'the style adapts itself to every modern necessity and convenience … I made no attempt to follow a particular style, the style grew naturally'.[37] Following established

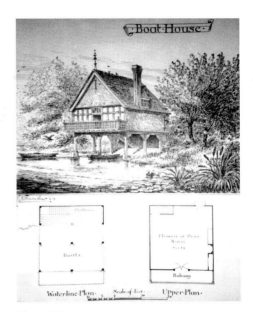

Figure 90
Boathouse in Shaw's book. His book demonstrates the great interest of Shaw and his contemporaries in new technology.[31] Ernest Newton, one of Shaw's pupils, published a companion volume, *Sketches for Country Residences* in 1882, with more Queen Anne style designs. (Courtesy of Nancy Sheiry Glaister.)

Fig. 100.—PAIR OF COTTAGES BUILT WITH CONCRETE ON MR. LASCELLES' SYSTEM.

Figure 91
Shirley Foster Murphy's *Our Homes and How to Keep Them Healthy*, 1883.

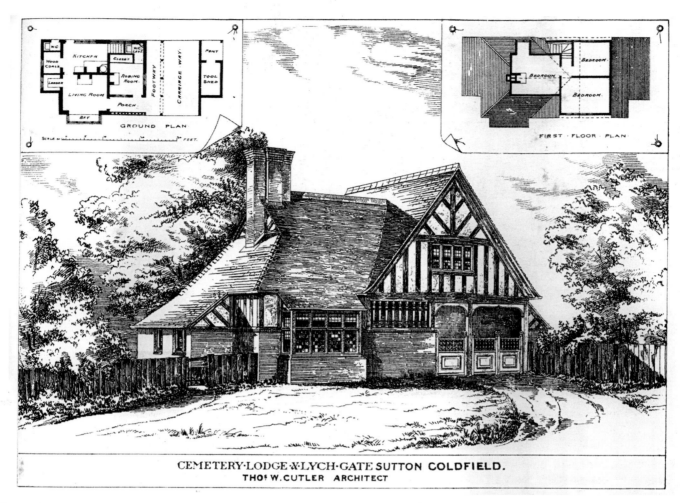

Figure 92
Cutler's cemetery lodge and lynch gate, Sutton Coldfield, *Building News*, 1880.

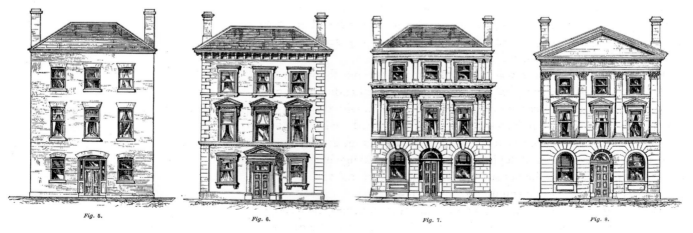

Figure 93
Common modes of obtaining architectural effect in the Classic style in Stevenson.

Figure 94
Draper's Almshouses, Margate, a source for the Queen Anne style.

practice was the key to success for speculative housebuilding and the style proved very popular;

> 'the London builder is adopting its features, with more chance of success than in Gothic, since it is the natural outcome of London materials and modes of work'.[38]

The second volume dealt with fashionable issues such as house planning and services, with a section on, for example, electric bells and speaking tubes. Stevenson followed Kerr's ideas on planning, with a list of ten characteristics, but there was a move away from compartmentalization to 'multifariousness', and a more modern simplified open house plan with fewer corridors, staircases and steps; such changes were underpinned by changing ideals in society generally by the late nineteenth century.[39]

The move to Queen Anne was also clear in cheap books for workmen; Brookes' popular *Rudimentary Treatise* of 1860 mentioned earlier, was in its seventh edition in 1896. A comparison of the 1860 edition with the 1896 edition reveals the broad sweep of change which had occurred – while the text, plans and back elevation are unchanged, the dramatic change in architectural fashions and the manner of depiction resulted in the change in the style of frontispiece of the front of the house from Italianate to Queen Anne, and tight shading to pen-and-ink style (Figures 95 and 96).

The growing number of building and architectural journals increasingly took over the role of the architectural pattern book, especially in the final few decades of the century. But the turn of the century and beyond sees a flurry of books about the small to medium house and its interior, and a number of

Figure 95
Back elevation used in Brookes' book of 1896 was the same as the 1860 edition.

Figure 96
Front elevation, in 1896 very differently depicted compared to 1860 edition.

books about cottages, which can here be only mentioned very briefly. Barry Parker and Raymond Unwin in *The Art of Building a Home*, 1901, stressed convenience and workability as the first consideration in designing a house. In contrast to the standard house plan, which was too divided up and cramped, and there are wasted rooms that are never used, 'Would it not be far better to reduce the number of rooms, keeping such rooms as we do retain, large enough to be healthy, comfortable, and habitable?' This book also commented on 'over decoration', stating that 'the average farmhouse has an artistic value far beyond that of ninety-nine out of every hundred drawing-rooms in the kingdom'.[40] Parker and Unwin's ideas can be traced back to Pugin and Morris, but they applied Arts and Crafts ideals to small houses, rather than middle-class houses. Maurice B. Adams' *Modern Cottage Architecture*, 1904, a pattern book of designs, which included his cottage designs at Bedford Park and Port Sunlight, and others by Shaw, Nesfield, Lutyens and Voysey, commented on the improvements in cottages of all kinds in the previous decade or so and drew attention to the evolution of the weekend cottage,[41] a reflection of wider changes in society towards a less formal lifestyle. The same year, the seminal work *Das Englische Haus* by Hermann Muthesius was published in Berlin, giving the first historical account of later Victorian British architecture and discussing in great detail the houses built by modern British architects such as Baillie Scott, C.R. Mackintosh and W.R. Lethaby.

REFERENCES

1 Eileen Harris, *British Architectural Books and Writers 1556–1785*, Cambridge University Press, 1990, 32.

2 John Archer, *The Literature of British Domestic Architecture 1715–1842*, The MIT Press, Cambridge, Mass. and London, 1985, 25.

3 see Dan Cruikshank and Peter Wyld, *Georgian Town Houses*, Butterworth Architecture, revised and reprinted edition, 1990.

4 David T. Yeomans, 'Early Carpenters' Manuals 1592–1820', *Journal of the Construction History Society,* volume 2, 1986, 18.

5 John Archer, *The Literature of British Domestic Architecture 1715–1842*, The MIT Press, Cambridge, Mass. and London, 1985, 11.

6 John Archer, *The Literature of British Domestic Architecture 1715–1842*, The MIT Press, Cambridge, Mass. and London, 1985, 29.

7 John Archer, *The Literature of British Domestic Architecture 1715–1842*, The MIT Press, Cambridge, Mass. and London, 1985, 12.

8 Iris Roderick Thomas, *Cyfarthfa and the Crawshays*, Rainbow Print (Wales) Ltd, 1999, 34.

9 Charles Parker, *Villa Rustica*, James Carpenter, London 1832–41, preface.

10 John Archer, *The Literature of British Domestic Architecture 1715–1842*, The MIT Press, Cambridge, Mass. and London, 1985, 102.

11 Henry Shaw, *Details of Elizabethan Architecture*, 1834, 1.

12 Paul Atterbury and Clive Wainwright, eds, *Pugin: a Gothic Passion*, Yale University Press, New Haven and London, in association with The Victoria and Albert Museum, 1994, 163.

13 John Archer, *The Literature of British Domestic Architecture 1715–1842*, The MIT Press, Cambridge, Mass. and London, 1985, 813 and 528.

14 Jane Loudon, *Gardening for Ladies*, John Murray, London, 1843, 444.

15 *The Architectural Magazine*, 1834, Cornmarket Reprints, London 1972, introduced by Ben Weinreb, n.p.

16 Jane Loudon, *Gardening for Ladies*, John Murray, London, 1843, 444.

17 *The Architectural Magazine*, 1834, 132.

18 Henry-Russell Hitchcock, *Early Victorian Architecture in Britain*, The Architectural Press, London: Yale University Press, New Haven, 1954, 425.

19 Henry-Russell Hitchcock, *Early Victorian Architecture in Britain*, The Architectural Press, London: Yale University Press, New Haven, 1954, 425.

20 Hermann Muthesius, *The English House*, BSP Professional Books, Oxford, 1987, 13.

21 For a detailed analysis, see Henry-Russell Hitchcock, *Early Victorian Architecture in Britain*, The Architectural Press, London: Yale University Press, New Haven, 1954, 428–30.

22 Robert Scott Burn, *The Grammar of House Planning*, John G. Murdoch, London, 1864, iii.

23 Robert Kerr, *The Gentleman's House*, John Murray, London, 1871, 49.

24 Robert, Kerr, *The Gentleman's House*, John Murray, London, 1871, 341.

25 Robert Kerr, *The Gentleman's House*, John Murray, London, 1871, 67.

26 W.J. and G.A. Audsley, *Cottage, Lodge and Villa Architecture*, Mackenzie, London, 1869, 1–23.

27 Blackie's *Villa and Cottage Architecture*, Blackie, London, 1868, vii-viii.

28 *Morning Post* in T Morris *A House for the Suburbs*, 1870, v.

29 Roger Dixon and Stefan Muthesius, *Victorian Architecture*, Thames and Hudson, London, 1978, 50.

30 Gillian Darley, *Villages of Vision*, The Architectural Press Ltd, London 1975, 113.

31 Priscilla Wrightson , *The Small English House*, B. Weinreb Architectural Books Ltd., London, 1977, 85.

32 J.J. Stevenson, *House Architecture*, Macmillan, London, 1880, 123.

33 J.J. Stevenson, *House Architecture*, Macmillan, London, 1880, 240.

34 J.J. Stevenson, *House Architecture*, Macmillan, London, 1880, 377.

35 J.J. Stevenson, *House Architecture*, Macmillan, London, 1880, 348.

36 J.J. Stevenson, *House Architecture*, Macmillan, London, 1880, 120.

37 J.J. Stevenson, *House Architecture*, Macmillan, London, 1880, 348.

38 J.J. Stevenson, *House Architecture*, Macmillan, London, 1880, 91.

39 see John Burnett, *A Social History of Housing 1815–1970*, Methuen and Co Ltd, London, 1980, 192.

40 Barry Parker and Raymond Unwin, *The Art of Building a Home*, Longmans, London, 1901, 3–5.

41 Maurice B. Adams, *Modern Cottage Architecture*, B.T. Batsford, London, 1904, preface.

3 Pattern books and manuals of Victorian exterior and interior details

For external and internal detailing, builders, architects, and clients could look to some of the architectural pattern books already mentioned. Some of the writers of architectural pattern books also wrote separately on interior fittings. These books similarly reflected the prevailing attitudes to style. Builders also consulted general builders' manuals which will be discussed later.

PATTERN BOOKS OF DESIGNS

There were also books of patterns for individual features or trades, such as cast iron and furniture. Some examples from this type of publication are given below. The origins of pattern books of design lie in textile model books of the early sixteenth century, and in the first comprehensive illustrated treatise on architecture by Sebastiano Serlio, published in six books between 1537 and 1551, which included patterns for ceilings and woodwork.[1] Later architectural writers already mentioned, such as Adam and Pain, included designs for all kinds of fittings and details, for example, ceilings, fireplaces and fanlights, in their works. Early books of patterns devoted to individual trades included Walter Gedde, *Sundry Draughts Principally Serving for Glaziers and Not Impertinent for Plasterers and Gardiners*, 1615–16 (reprinted in the nineteenth century by Henry Shaw), which had 180 designs for leaded windows, John Carwithen, *Floor Decorations of Various kinds … Adapted to the Ornamenting of Halls, Rooms, Summer Houses etc.*, 1739, a collection of 24 designs, each showing a design and its effect *in situ*, and John Crunden, *The Joyner and Cabinet-Maker's Darling or Pocket Director*, 1765, consisting of 40 designs for 'Gothic, Mosaic, and Ornamental Frets', and 20 designs for fanlights.

Early ironwork pattern books included those by Jean Tijou (1693) and Jean Berain (1700), and Isaac Ware was the first to claim that 'cast iron is very serviceable to the builder and a vast expense is saved in many cases in using it'.[2] Builders, founders and so on, wishing to work with cast iron, a material which was so important for the insides and outsides of Victorian houses, looked to two pattern books on cast iron in particular in the early Victorian period written by antiquarians; L.N. Cottingham, *The Ornamental Metal Worker's Director*, 1823, reprinted in 1840, was the first nineteenth-century book to satisfy a need for such patterns,[3] aiming 'to remove in some measure the severe and painful regret that has long been felt by ingenious workmen, for the want of a collection of good ornaments to select from, at a price within the compass of their limited means'. Cottingham covered 'every class of building' from the palace to the 'social villa

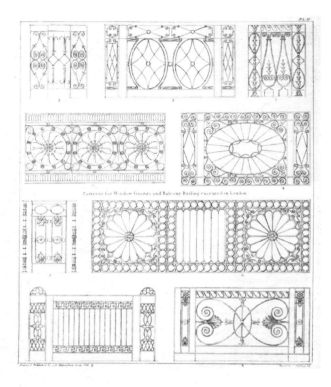

Figure 97
Cottingham's designs for verandahs, fences, balcony, area and window guards. The bottom right-hand design was particularly popular, appearing in London, Cheltenham, Leamington Spa and Tenby. (Courtesy of RIBA Library Photographs Collection.)

of the retired citizen', with 82 designs and patterns by 'the most eminent artists … as may be a guide to [artisans and tradesmen] in forming correct and tasteful compositions', for example, John Nash, and also based on his personal museum collection. Designs included stoves and fenders for drawing rooms, 'serviceable to ladies and gentlemen to select from, and equally so the furnishing ironmonger'. Cottingham's designs were much copied by founders and appear all over Britain, and as far afield as America and Australia (Figure 97).[4] The other influential early Victorian pattern book of designs for staircases, railings, etc. was *Examples of Ornamental Metalwork*, by Henry Shaw, 1836, containing 50 designs by Shaw and prominent architects such as Sidney Smirke.

Many of these books were aimed specifically at the trade for workmen to copy. W.F. Pocock's *Modern Finishings for Rooms*, 1811, 1823, 1837, contained detailed designs of doors, windows, chimney-pieces, cornices and other finishings for every room in the house, 'according to the methods of the best workmen in London'. Designs, often reproduced full scale, were specifically intended to help country workmen on how to best follow the 'prevailing fashions'. The book also addressed 'Gentlemen … whose situation prevents their having the aid of an architect, may with confidence proceed in the finishing [of] their houses according to the designs here shown'. Similarly, E.W. Trendall's *Examples for Interior Finishings*, 1833, 14s, was aimed at 'all persons connected with the practical parts of the building', with lithographed plates of folding doors, French windows, staircases, chimney-pieces, and 'cornices for rooms and staircases and other mouldings drawn to full size'; it was 'useful … for carpenters and builders' according to *The Architectural Magazine* which added that as this book published details in the classical or 'modern' style, equivalent books on the Gothic and Elizabethan styles would be useful.[5] For a wider popular market, Loudon's *Encyclopaedia* contained much on interior fittings, including cornice mouldings, ceiling roses, paint, wallpaper, and fireplaces (Figures 98 and 101).

With the popularity of the numbers trade in publishing, publications were becoming more accessible. *A Compilation of Splendid Ornamental Designs, from Foreign Works of Recent Production. Adapted for the study of Drawing, to assist the artist and decorator, and to aid in the various manufactures where superior ornament is required*, was sold every fortnight, in parts, eight altogether with three plates each, at 1s per part. Loudon's *Architectural Magazine* said 'we hail the work as the commencement of an era of good and cheap architectural publications, which workmen may afford to purchase, as well as architects'.[6]

The changes in styles of interior furnishing can be plotted through the pattern books (and later journals and trade catalogues) for the trade. To give a very brief resumé of some important books, an early example is Thomas Sheraton's *Cabinet Dictionary* of 1803, primarily a manual, but with many designs that he indicated could be copied. His list of subscribers was almost exclusively cabinet makers and joiners (Figure 99). Sheraton's designs linked Adam to Thomas Hope, a wealthy connoisseur, who first used the term 'interior decoration'.[7] His book, *Household Furniture and Interior Decoration* executed from designs by Thomas Hope, was based on his travels round the Mediterranean and his personal collection and served as the main source for Neoclassicism. J.C. Loudon was inspired by his home, Deepdene, near Dorking, which he visited in 1829. Neoclassicism was prolonged by writers like Peter Nicholson. He had been a cabinet maker before moving onto architecture, and his book, *The Practical Cabinet Maker, Upholsterer and Complete Decorator*, 1826–7, sixth edition 1846, was 'a complete treatise … the designs made clearly intelligible to the gentleman and the amateur'. The pictures included interior schemes, beds, chairs, tables, curtains, wardrobes. Most designs were in the Neoclassical style, with a few Egyptian and Gothic designs added.

The challenge to Neoclassicism from other styles can be seen in the works of Thomas King, author of over 20 books, notably, *The Modern Style of Cabinet Work Exemplified*, 1829, reissued to 1862, which included Old French (or rococo) designs which were easily copied using composition. His patterns, drawn from manufacturers' designs of the time, were further disseminated through the popular Webster's *Encyclopaedia of Domestic Economy*, 1844, destined for the middle-class home.[8] Richard Brown's *Rudiments of Drawing Cabinet and Upholstery Furniture*, 1820, contained a new style, of heavy, rounded forms and carving that added essential ingredients of ornamentation and comfort, forming the look of the Victorian interior. Further contributions to

Figure 98
Designs for ceiling enrichments in Loudon's book.

Figure 99
Plate from Sheraton's *Cabinet Dictionary*.

the style debate came from Henry Shaw's *Ornamental Works in Louis XIV's Style*, 1833 and *Specimens of Ancient Furniture*, 1835, sold in parts, 5s each, from A.C. Pugin, *Gothic Furniture*, 1827, previously published in *Ackermann's Repository*, 1825–7, and from Pugin's *Gothic Furniture*, 1835, a serious study of Gothic which was to become very influential on later writers (Figure 100). Loudon's *Encyclopaedia*, summarizing the style debate for a wider public, identified four main styles for furniture in 1833: Grecian, Gothic, Tudor or Elizabethan, and Louis Quatorze. His book included furnishing for all classes of house, in contrast to other books which focused on the middle- and upper-class interior, and dealt with new materials and technologies.

The increasing stylistic eclecticism in interiors and furniture by the 1850s can be seen in Blackie's, *The Cabinet-Maker's Assistant*, 1853, probably written by P. Thompson.[9] This was a much copied manual and pattern book aimed at the trade, covering drawing, woods, and a vast range of patterns for furniture, cornice mouldings, etc. and included designs taken from the Great Exhibition of 1851. The upholstered and tasselled interior of the middle-class home, while remaining a status symbol for many, was under threat as heavy, rounded forms were replaced by rectilinear shapes of art furniture from the late 1860s. A prominent figure in the transmission of this new mood to a more popular audience was Scottish architect, Bruce J. Talbert, author of two books, both of which were reprinted in Boston, Massachusetts, USA.[10]

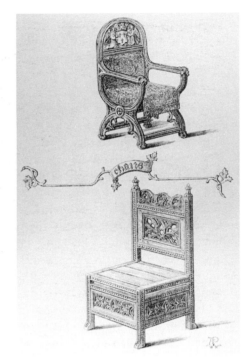

Figure 100
Designs for chairs from *Gothic Furniture*, 1835. (Courtesy of Architectural Resource Centre, Cardiff University.)

1847

1848 is a Design for a chimney-piece in the style of Louis XIV,

1848

Figure 101
Fireplace in Louis XIV style.

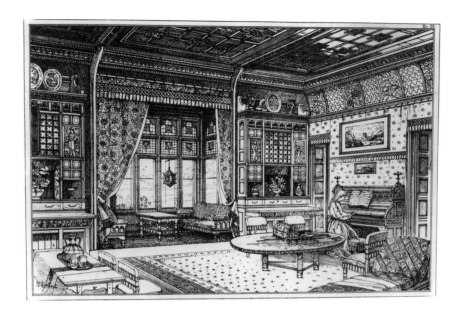

Figure 102
Plate from *Gothic Forms*. (V & A Picture Library)

Talbert's first book, *Gothic Forms Applied to Furniture, Metal-work and Decoration for Domestic Purposes*, 1867 (Figure 102), echoed Eastlake's approach in *Hints on Household Taste,* republished from articles in the *Cornhill Magazine*. Central to Talbert was the question of honesty in furniture construction,

> 'the best isolated efforts of the Architectural profession can do little to render this class of furniture popular, until the cabinet-maker and his workmen take some interest in their work'.

Talbert's second pattern book, *Examples of Ancient and Modern Furniture, Metalwork, Tapestries, Decoration etc.*, 1876 demonstrated how much taste had changed since 1867 under the influence of the Queen Anne style; he described how once thirteenth century Gothic admirers now turned to Tudor, Jacobean or Georgian, even Rococo, and recalled earlier works of Henry Shaw and T.F. Hunt.[11] There was a useful historical table to guide readers through style, listing styles and main domestic works from 1399 to 1830, from Perpendicular, Tudor and Elizabethan, Jacobean (including Italian Renaissance), to Georgian.

An essential ingredient of the aesthetic interior was the influence of Japan, first introduced to Britain in the early 1860s. In particular, it appears in the simple, lightweight, rectilinear furniture of E.W. Godwin, who published a pattern book, *Art Furniture*, 1877, with manufacturer, William Watt. Victorian books on ornament is a separate large area of study and cannot be included here in detail, but it should be briefly noted that there were a number of books on ornament by writers who were particularly interested in Japanese art, for example, the Audsley brothers and Thomas Cutler issued important books on Japanese ornament in 1875 and 1880, respectively. Most notable was Christopher Dresser's *Studies in Design*, 1874–6, which aimed at decorators, householders, designers and manufacturers, to 'bring about a better style of decoration for our houses'. It contained 60 chromolithographed plates of designs for ceilings, walls and dadoes, drawing on a range of influences from Japanese, Persian and Indian art to stylized plant forms, and was the key book of patterns for interior decoration.[12] The Aesthetic style was transmitted to a wide public through journals, trade catalogues and manuals of home decoration and was much imitated on a variety of levels, from whole schemes in Queen Anne style houses, to Japanese fans and blue and white china advocated in many manuals (depending on one's budget) as a means of lending a fashionable look to the ordinary home.

TRADE MANUALS AND PRICE BOOKS

Practical written advice on housebuilding and decoration was available from manuals, both general building and those specific to one trade. That many of the books were reissued over many years shows the need for such books, and the conservatism of the building industry and Victorian tastes generally. First-ly, price books gave prices for materials and labour, reproduced Building Acts and included outline elevations and plans for terraced houses according to the four rates of house, which were generally omitted from early Victorian pattern books (Figures 103 and 104).

FRONTISPIECE TO THE PRACTICAL BUILDER'S PRICE BOOK.

DESIGN FOR A CASTELLATED VILLA.

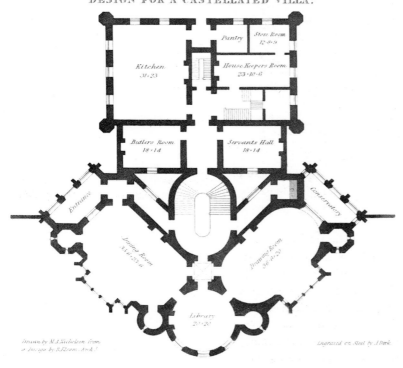

Figure 103
This same frontispiece appeared in Kelly's price books of 1825, 1841 and 1863. (Courtesy of V & A Picture Library.)

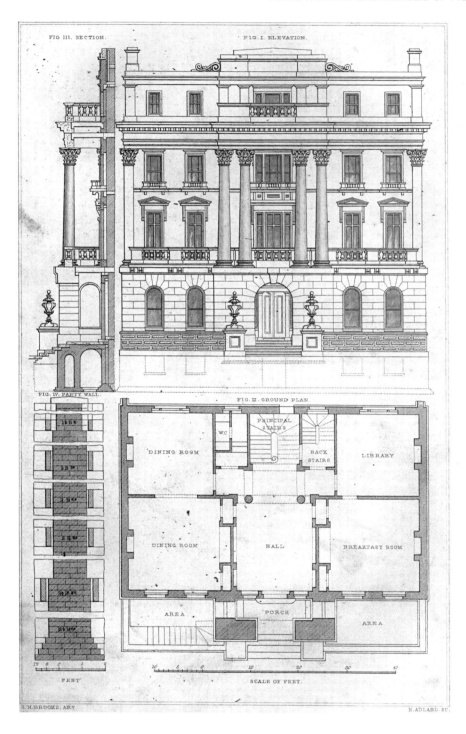

Figure 104
First-rate house in Kelly's price book of 1863.

Books to aid the builder in measuring of building works (before quantity surveying), and price books with up-to-date prices for labour and materials to
protect workmen,[13] had been introduced in the eighteenth century. I. & J.
Taylor's *Builders Price Book* first appeared in 1776, and Laxton's price books
began in 1826. Price books expanded in size over the years to cater for increasingly diversified trades and new materials and products, as can be seen from
a comparison of Richard Elsam's *The Practical Builder's Perpetual Price Book*,
Kelly, 1841 edition, and H. Laxton's *The Builder's Price Book*, 71st edition, 1888;

Figure 105
Designs for cottages in John Blenkarn, civil engineer and architect, *Practical Specifications of Works*, executed in architecture, civil and mechanical engineering, and in roadmaking and sewering, 1865, aimed at young architects.

Elsam covered the work of carpenters and joiners, sawyers, bricklayers and masons, plasterers, slaters, plumbers, painters, glaziers and smiths; Laxton's book of 1888 added blind manufacturer, gilder and paperhanger, sanitary work, bell-hanger, gas fitter and electrical work, ironmonger, engineer, to the list, with the conventional trades themselves subdivided into different specialisms. Rapidly changing fashions meant that styles, prices and other information contained in such publications could not remain accurate, and price books were from the 1870s increasingly superseded by the trade catalogue. The first book of specifications was Alfred Bartholomew's (later briefly editor of *The Builder*) *Specifications for Practical Architecture*, an essay on the decline of excellence in the structure and in the science of modern English buildings, 1840. The work was intended to give exact descriptions

'which are requisite for the contracting for and manipulation of buildings … more than twenty years ago, I began this description of technical literature, I found prevalent in it a coarse style of vagueness, which … left ample room upon a thousand points for Builders to exercise imagination as to the intentions of the writers of it.'[14]

The eighteenth-century builder's manuals of Price, Pain and so on mentioned in Chapter 2, were transformed by Peter Nicholson who set a new standard, look and tone for building manuals in the nineteenth century. He wrote 24 books over a period from 1782 to 1837, whose content ranged widely, from furniture as we have already seen, to carpentry and architecture. Nicholson's books were very popular, *The Carpenter's New Guide*, 1792, was in its thirteenth edition by 1857. His main contribution lay in his new high standard of detailed scientific and technical writing, essential in an age of rising importance of the engineer and new types of buildings, methods of construction and materials. In particular, his contributions in the fields of roof construction and hand railing (for which the Society of Arts awarded him its gold medal in 1814), and the inclusion of instruction on doors and their hinges, and windows and shutters, served to set his books apart from earlier works.[15]

His most well-known work, *The New Practical Builder and Workmen's Companion*, 1823, republished through to 1861 (Figures 106–110), aimed to teach the art of building to the professional and the 'untaught', and was explained in a consciously straightforward way. The book contained a series of designs 'in the modern style', for 'the various ranks of society', and boasted 'a much greater variety of subjects than any similar work … and … many things entirely new … for example, in the design of roofs, several modes are brought forward for the first time'. Nicholson stressed the importance of geometry,

> 'The execution of the design of the architect is generally left to the skill of the workmen … if he be not practically acquainted with the geometrical construction of the object to be executed, he is not only unfit for the undertaking, but, at every step that he takes, he will manifest his ignorance and inability, and eventually overwhelm himself with confusion and disgrace'.

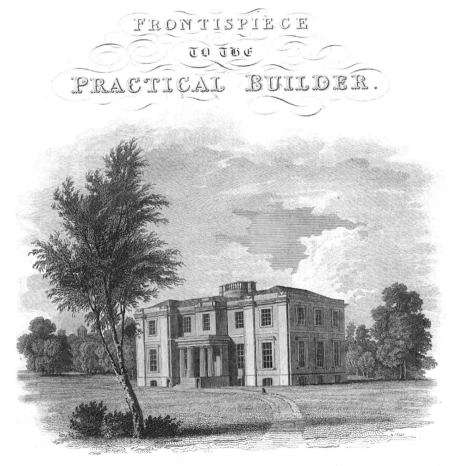

THE HOUSE OF FULTON ALEXANDER ESQ.ᴿ
at Patrick near Glasgow

Figure 106
Frontispiece to Nicholson's book. This copy was owned by Thomas Powell, carpenter, Builth Wells, October 1830.

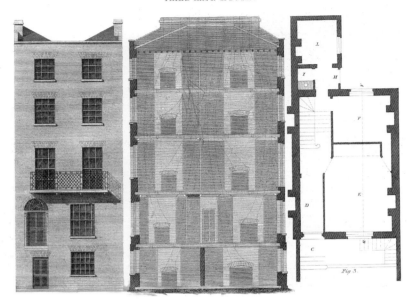

THIRD-RATE HOUSE.

Figure 107
A third-rate house in Nicholson.

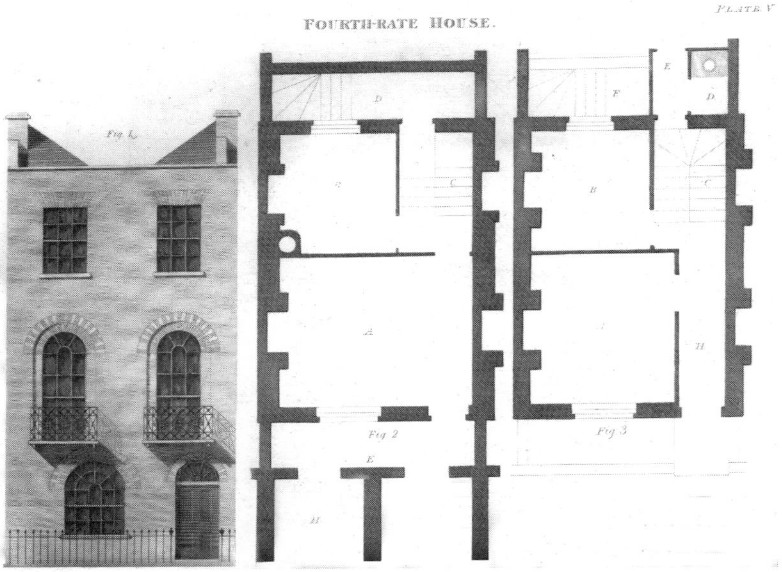

FOURTH-RATE HOUSE.

Figure 108
A fourth-rate house.

Figure 109
Grecian mouldings in Nicholson.

The many different revised and retitled versions of Nicholson's work in later years can be attributed to his failed monthly journal *The School of Architecture and Engineering*, which lasted only five issues, obliging him to sell the rights of earlier work. One of the main writers who revised Nicholson was Thomas Tredgold, who published *The New and Improved Practical Builder*, in 1861, and *Practical Carpentry, Joinery and Cabinet Making*, from 1849 to 1857. Tredgold's own work, *Elementary Principles of Carpentry*, first published 1820, became a standard work for the second half of the century, to be republished, with many editions in the 1880s, through to 1919. Tredgold, also wrote a book on warming and ventilation in 1824. His work shows how building books were beginning to branch out into diverse trades and engineering.[16]

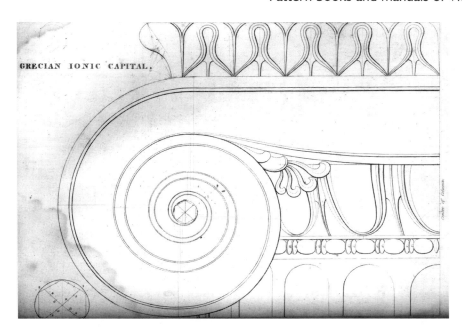

Figure 110
Full-page design which had clearly been used as a practical aid. 'The schemes or diagrams are proportioned in their size to their probable utility'.

Tredgold's *Elementary Principles of Carpentry* was part of an cheap technical series aimed at a mass market, Weale's *Rudimentary, Scientific and Educational* series, which won a prize medal at the 1862 International Exhibition. In 1868, its titles included *Cottage Building, The Drainage of Towns and Buildings*, and several standard works by architect Edward Dobson, including *Rudiments of the Art of Building*, 1849, in its sixteenth edition in 1923, and *A Rudimentary Treatise on the Manufacture of Bricks and Tiles*, 1850, in its fourth edition in 1936 (Figure 5). Towards the end of the century (and increasingly after 1900) there were many other affordable manuals brought out, partly or entirely aimed at the emerging do-it-yourself amateur carpenter market (Figure 112).

Plasterers, masons and related trades were often grouped together, as in F. Reinnel's *Masons, Bricklayers, Plasterers and Slaters' Assistant*, first published 1834, perhaps a reflection of the extent of overlapping of trades especially outside London. Larger and more elaborate volumes appear, catering for the needs of running up suburban houses, for example, *The Mason's, Bricklayer's, Plasterer's and Decorator's Practical Guide*, Hagger, 1859–62, edited by E.L. Blackburne and 'assisted by eminent architects and builders'. With many full-page illustrations of scrolled brackets and cornice and ceiling mouldings, its Italianate detailing was widely copied. Robert Scott Burn's (editor), *The New Guide to Masonry Bricklaying and Plastering. Theoretical and Practical*, 1868–72, was written a decade later along similar lines (Figures 113–116). It was a large volume:

'Within the last few years and original, bold, and comprehensive practice has been opened up in Britain, as well as on the Continent of Europe and in America, in the various branches of the building Arts, with fresh adaptations of materials and with ingenious appliances. A work therefore which shall present these most recent improvements … has now become an obvious necessity to the proper instruction of the modern mechanic … recent architectural adaptations and structural novelties, in terracotta and artificial stone work – important, little availed of, yet cheap and effective sources of architectural ornamentation … make it the most comprehensive and exhaustive treatise to be issued'.

He wrote a companion volume, *New Guide to Carpentry*, 1868–72.

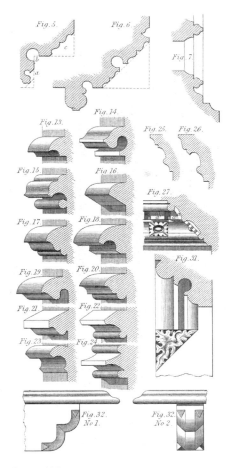

Figure 111
Plate from a prominent authority on carpentry in the second half of the nineteenth century, James Newlands, *The Carpenter and Joiner's Assistant*, 1857–60, still in demand 20 years later.

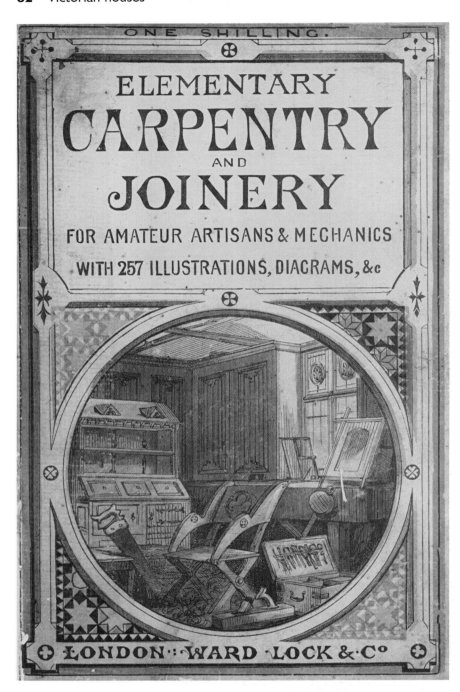

ONE SHILLING.

ELEMENTARY
CARPENTRY
AND
JOINERY
FOR AMATEUR ARTISANS & MECHANICS
WITH 257 ILLUSTRATIONS, DIAGRAMS, &c

LONDON :: WARD LOCK & Cº

Figure 112
Elementary Carpentry and Joinery for Amateur Artisans and Mechanics, published by Ward Lock & Co, price 1s. Ward Lock brought out other books along similar lines, such as *Every Man His Own Mechanic*, 1880.

Finally, in 1897, a weighty guide exclusively dedicated to the plaster trade covering the history and current practice and trade of plastering, William Millar's *Plastering Plain and Decorative*, appeared (Figure 117).

To mention a few other trades, early nineteenth-century writers on interior decoration included Nathaniel Whittock, *The Decorative Painters' and Glaziers' Guide*, 1827, notable for some coloured lithographs representing woods, whereby the 'effect of colour and polish obtained by first painting the lithograph with bright watercolours and then covering with a solution of gum arabic used as varnish'. At roughly the same time, D.R. Hay, 'house painter' of Edinburgh, published *On the Laws of Harmonious Colouring, adapted to Interior Decorations, Manufacturers, and Other Useful Purposes*, 1828, sixth edition

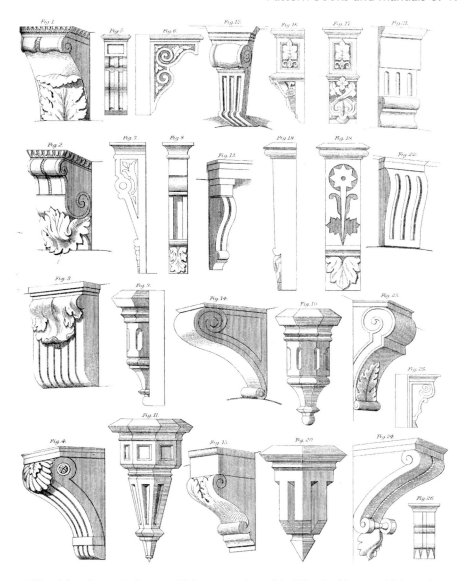

Figure 113
Brackets in Scott Burn's book.

1847, with coloured plates, which was reviewed in *The Architectural Magazine*:

> 'One of the characteristics of the present age is, the union of science and practice in our tradesmen and manufacturers every young architect, builder, or other person connected with houses or furniture … may gain [much] from Mr Hay's book'.[17]

The firm of H.W. & A. Arrowsmith were well established on fashionable New Bond Street, and were decorators to Queen Victoria; in 1840 they published a manual/pattern book, *The House Decorator and Painters Guide*, still in print 20 years later, which had many hand-coloured plates of room schemes in styles of the 1830s and 1840s, for example, Elizabethan, Greek and Roman revival, and 'modern French'. They commented that in contemporary practice Gothic and Elizabethan were frequently intermixed, and 'we see the different styles of Gothic … mingled together, and forming an indescribable mass'. A later, cheaper and more purely practical manual with few pictures was E.A. Davidson's, *House Painting, Graining and Marbling*, 1876, which remained a standard text after 1900. After 1900 the market was inundated with small manuals aimed at house painters appeared on various aspects of housepainting, and in particular, stencilling, and painter's books of business and specifications, for example Cassell's 'work' handbooks.

Figure 114
Brickwork patterns.

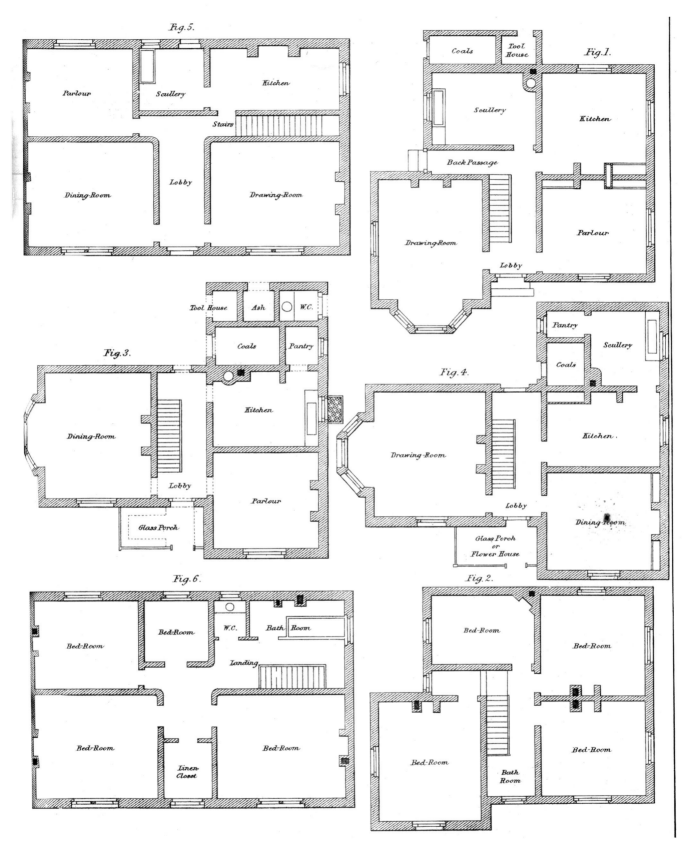

Figure 115
House plans, economically shown all on one page.

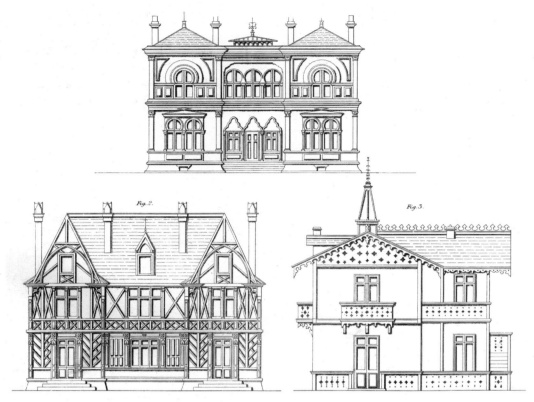

Figure 116
A range of typical house styles presented on a single page in Scott Brown.

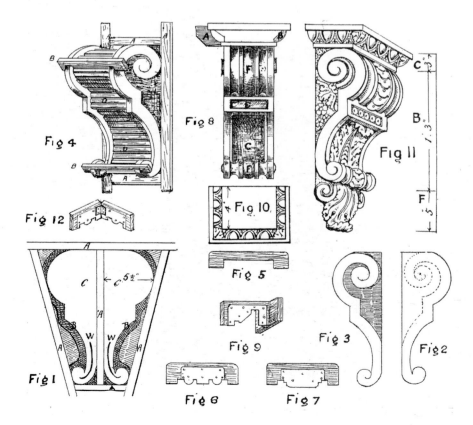

Figure 117
Plaster moulding in Millar's book.

'Italian villa style' semi, £340 each house, demonstrated prevalently conservative taste (Figure 84).

House in Bedford Park (Figure 88). (David Long)

TERRACE HOUSE, SHOWING FOUNDATIONS AND DRAINAGE.

A. Ventilating shaft for air inlet and access to drain. | CC. Drain enclosed in concrete. | E. Yard gully. | G. Shaft for access to upper end of drain.
B. Syphon traps. | D. Open pipe for bath waste. | F. Soil pipe carried up above eaves, as ventilating shaft. | HH. Ventilating damp-proof course.

Terraced house, showing foundations and drainage (Figure 119).

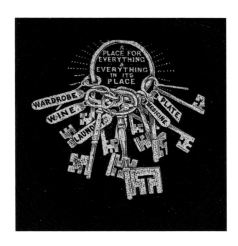

Cover of *A Practical Housewife* (Figure 121).

MODERN MANTEL PIECE, WITH LACE ON VELVET DROP.

A fireplace arrangement from *A Manual of Domestic Economy, Suited to Families Spending from £100 to 1000 a Year*, by J.H. Walsh, 1879 edition (Figure 122).

Advice on window gardening in Cassell's *Household Guide* (Figure 123).

WINDOW GARDENING.

Bay window display in Beeton's *New Book of Garden Management*, c.1890 (Figure 124).

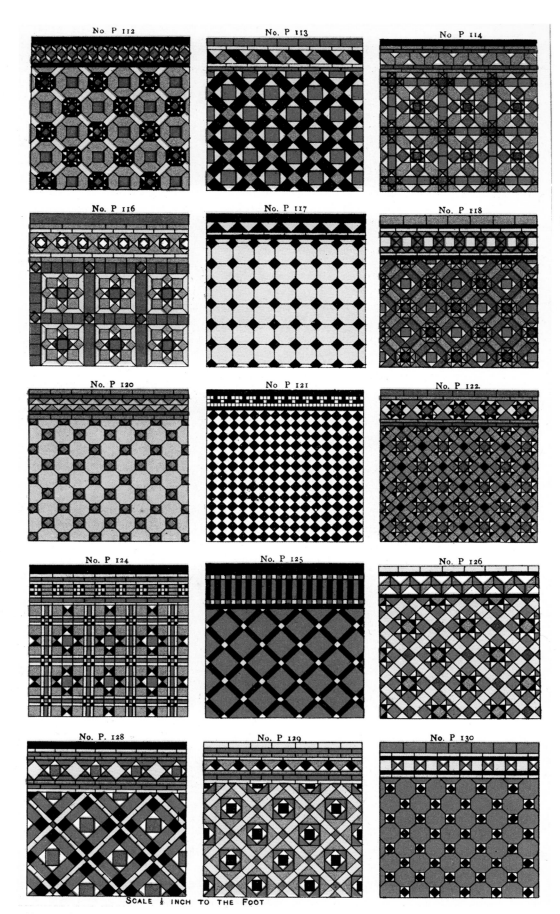

No P 112   No P 113   No P 114
No. P 116   No. P 117   No. P 118
No. P 120   No P 121   No. P 122
No. P 124   No. P 125   No. P 126
No. P. 128   No. P 129   No. P 130

SCALE ½ INCH TO THE FOOT

Young and Marten floor tiles (Figure 144).

P3165. THE "ROLLARGIO" ROMAN SHAPE BATH

P1559. THE "CASCADIO" ROMAN SHAPE BATH

P4458. THE "VALORIO" ROMAN SHAPE BATH

Prices of these Baths quoted upon application,

Choice of baths in Young and Marten's catalogue (Figure 145).

Design for a fountain in *Ackermann's Repository of the Arts* in 1819 (Figure 147).

Issues surrounding heating, plumbing and ventilation attracted great attention in the periodical and non-periodical press throughout the Victorian period, with interests shifting from solving problems of heating houses, to plumbing and lighting. In addition to the attention paid to these issues in architectural books already mentioned, there were also many individual treatises on these subjects for the trade, in addition to examples already cited by Tredgold and Richardson, key authors also included Charles Hood (1837), N. Arnott (1855), Frederick Edwards (1868), T. Pridgin Teale (1883) and Douglas Galton (1884). The standard text on plumbing, published as the public became alerted to the subject when the Prince of Wales nearly died from typhoid, was S.S. Hellyer's *The Plumber and Sanitary Houses*, 1877, fifth edition 1893 (Figure 118).

FIG. 147.—"Optimus" (G) Valve-closet with Whiteware Front and Sides, isolated from the Side Walls.

Figure 118
Optimus valve closet from Hellyer's book.

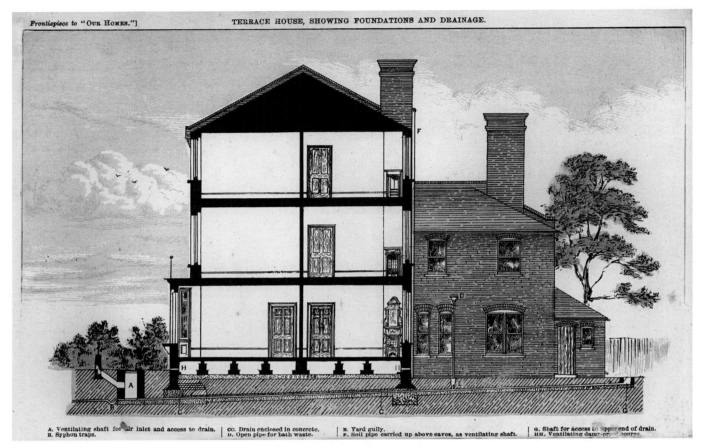

A. Ventilating shaft for air inlet and access to drain. | CC. Drain enclosed in concrete. | E. Yard gully. | G. Shaft for access to upper end of drain.
B. Syphon traps. | D. Open pipe for bath waste. | F. Soil pipe carried up above eaves, as ventilating shaft. | HH. Ventilating damp-proof course.

Figure 119
Terraced house, showing foundations and drainage.

The interest in sanitation and hygiene was associated with aesthetic movement lightweight, moveable furniture and furnishings. Shirley Foster Murphy, vice-president of Royal Sanitary Institute, edited *Our Homes and How to Make Them Healthy*, 1883, with sections on architecture, internal decoration, lighting, warming and ventilation, drainage and house cleaning, among others, written by 16 experts, including Douglas Galton and Robert W. Edis (Figure 119).

The International Health Exhibition of 1884 raised the profile of this subject, and issued a number of handbooks by specialists, for example, Edis' *Healthy Furniture and Decoration*, 1884. Demand for the latest information in a rapidly changing situation led to G. Lister Sutcliffe (editor), *The Principles and Practice of Modern House Construction*, 1898–9, to make rapidly available all the most advanced practical information, with contributions from 17 experts, including Robert Kerr. Sutcliffe was the second architect at Brentham Garden Suburb, begun 1901, and contributed designs for 1500 houses there and elsewhere.[18] New inventions resulted in new trades, each with their specific publications, such as R. Hammond's *Electric Lighting in Our Homes*, 1890, and F.C. Allsopp's *Practical Electric Bell Fitting*, 1899.

DECORATION AND HOME MANUALS

The final quarter of the nineteenth century saw particular expansion in manuals on home decoration aimed at householders, particularly women, rather than the building trades. Information on this subject was previously found in pattern books, such as Loudon's.

Early precursors to later popular manuals on home furnishing, *included How to keep House or Comfort and Elegance on £150 to £200 a Year*, sixth edition 1832. The author recommended 'If London be the domicile of the persons who read this, I should advise then to avoid the following neighbourhoods', and gave a long list including, 'any of the small tenements about the lower end of Sloane Street', 'any of the streets between Tottenham Court Road and Gower Street', ' the streets leading from Euston Square to Hampstead', and 'all Bayswater'. The best houses of an average kind in London the author judged to include Paddington, Kensington, parts of Islington, Kentish Town, Hackney, Brixton and Clapham. Readers were advised that:

> 'RATS and MICE, heavy TAXES of all kinds, the want of convenient CLOSETS, indifferent FLOORING, a KITCHEN below, and dingy loose PAPERING come under the head of nuisances, that ought to be shunned either wholly or in great part.'[19]

Aimed at the middle classes with servants, was Mrs Beeton's famous *Book of Household Management*, 1861, costing 7s 6d, which had first appeared in 1859 in monthly parts in her husband's magazine, *The Englishwoman's Domestic Magazine*. The second biggest seller after the Holy Bible, it sold nearly two million copies by 1868, and in the 1870s, its publishers, Ward Lock, were running off 20,000 in an edition.[20] Other manuals of domestic economy included *A Practical Housewife*, first published 1855 (Figure 121), *Household Hints; or, How to Make a Home Happy*, by William Jones, c.1860, and *A Manual of Domestic Economy, Suited to Families Spending from £100 to 1000 a Year*, by J.H. Walsh, first published 1859 (Figure 122).

Walsh's book was a comprehensive manual on cookery, all aspects of the home, including buying and renting a house, building and planning, warming, ventilating and lighting, finishing and furnishing. Walsh commented that 'architects' and builders' bills are so often sore subjects in families', explaining how it was common practice for architects to deliberately run up extra costs on a £1000 house, because at their fee of 5% of the total cost, payment of £50 was too little for all the work involved in drawing up plans and superintending building work, though Walsh felt this was 'a very lame apology'.[21] Furniture prices were given by Walsh for furnishing a range of houses according to price lists of W.S. Burton, Oxford Street and Messrs Atkinson & Co, Westminster. A house with four bedrooms and three servants' bedrooms, with an income of £1500, would total £1701 5s 1d; a £750-income house with three reception rooms and three bedrooms with servants could have furniture costing £670 18s 6d; a £350-income house with two reception-roomed house with two main bedrooms, a servant's bedrooms and a children's room would cost £192 14s 10d to furnish, while an income of £150 could not afford a whole house in London but in the countryside, furniture expenditure for a two bedroomed house with kitchen and parlour would total £63 16s 8d.[22]

A trend towards multi-volumed comprehensive guides to the home, which accelerated after 1900, began with Cassell's *Book of the Household*, four volumes, 1868, which gave advice on choosing a home, its furnishing, decorating, running, the care of the children, the garden and home entertainment (Figure 123). Beeton capitalized on the demand for publications with a series of cheap guides on a range of subjects, including gardening. Gardening books

Figure 120
Curtain arrangement in *Hints on Houses and House Furnishing*, 1851. This was a small book with a Gothic-style binding, mostly detailed text with a few outline drawings of bedsteads, dressers, etc. and aimed at a young market.

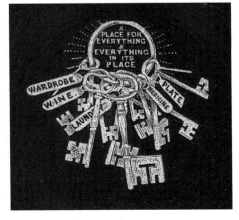

Figure 121
Cover of *A Practical Housewife*.

MODERN MANTEL PIECE, WITH LACE ON VELVET DROP.

Figure 122
A fireplace arrangement from *A Manual of Domestic Economy, Suited to Families Spending from £100 to 1000 a Year*, by J.H. Walsh, 1879 edition.

and journals first became popular in the eighteenth century, for example, John Abercrombie's *Every Man his Own Gardener*, in its eighteenth edition in 1805. Among the most popular authors were Jane Loudon with books such as *Lady's Companion to the Flower Garden*, 1841, which ran to nine editions and sold 20,000 copies,[23] and Shirley Hibberd with *Rustic Adornments for Homes of Taste*, 1856, which had early examples of chromolithographed plates.

One of the most influential books specifically on home decoration and furnishing was architect Charles Eastlake's *Hints on Household Taste*, 1867, which cost 18s and was compiled from his articles in the *Cornhill Magazine*. Eastlake and Mrs Beeton were the two best-known books of the 1860s.[24] This book played a huge role in popularizing a version of Pugin's Gothic of the 1840s for the middle classes, with an emphasis on rectilinearity, craftsmanship and painted decoration, which was also publicized by Bruce Talbert (Figure 125). It also contained chomolithographed plates of designs for wallpapers, and tiled and parquetry floors by the well-known manufacturers, Maw & Co, and H.J. Arrowsmith. It ran to four editions in Britain and to six editions in the USA, and became so familiar

Figure 123
Advice on window gardening in Cassell's *Household Guide*.

WINDOW GARDENING.

Figure 124
Bay window display in Beeton's *New Book of Garden Management*, c.1890.

Mantel-piece Shelves,
executed from a Design by Charles L. Eastlake.

Figure 125
Mantel-piece shelves in Eastlake's book.

that interiors done out in this style were said to have been 'Eastlaked'. He went on to write a history of the Gothic revival in 1872, at the point of major change in architectural style.[25]

The Aesthetic movement sparked a new interest among a wide public, particularly the middle classes, in interior decoration and furnishing. Responding to the general interest in 'artistic' taste, between 1876 and 1878 Macmillan issued the cheap 'Art at Home' series, which included Lady Barker, *The Bedroom and the Boudoir*, 1878, and Mrs Orrinsmith's *The Drawing Room*, 1877 at 2s 6d each (Figure 126). Mrs Loftie's *The Dining Room*, 1878 was:

'not intended for people who can afford to employ skilled decorators, nor yet for those who can give costly entertainments. It merely contains a few practical

Figure 126
'Art at Home' motif.

Frontispiece.

A·Drawing·Room·Corner·   R.W.EDIS, F.S.A. ARCHT ⊕

Figure 127
Frontispiece to architect R.W. Edis' *Decoration and Furnishing of Town Houses*, 1881. (Courtesy of V & A Picture Library.)

suggestions for inexperienced housekeepers of small income, who do not wish to make limited means an excuse for disorder and ugliness'.[26]

R.W. Edis was president of the Architectural Association and designer of houses in London. Drawn from a series of lectures to the Society of Arts in 1880, his book, *Decoration and Furnishing of Town Houses*, 1881, aimed to show

'what can be done to improve the general dreariness of an ordinary Town House, by a little thought and a conscientious regard for use and comfort, combined with artistic design, arrangement and moderate expense'.

In particular, he emphasized integrated and economic, well-made schemes, where design was used to eliminate dust traps in bedrooms and nurseries[27] (Figure 126).

The Art of Decoration, 1882, by the well-known writer, Mrs Haweis, was followed by her book, *Beautiful Houses*, comprising descriptions of well-known artistic houses, which appeared originally in the *Queen*, 1880–1, and including houses belonging to Sir Frederick Leighton, William Burges, and J.J. Stevenson (Figure 128). Her position was clear:

'Without holding up any particular style as proper for imitation … it is serviceable to show that … every style has a beauty and interest of its own … No house, no picture, no piece of music, is interesting or instructive which is a servile copy of something else'.

Of Burges' house at 9 Melbury Road, London, she commented:

'Mr Burges is perhaps our best authority on mediaeval architecture and decoration; and his own house is built on mediaeval precedent, even to the thirteenth century round tower which marks it, and it is a forcible protest against fashionable gloom.'[28]

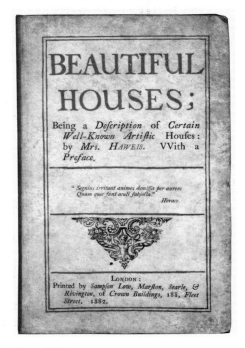

BEAUTIFUL HOUSES;

Being a *Description* of *Certain Well-Known Artistic* Houses : by *Mrs. HAWEIS.* With a *Preface.*

" *Segnius irritant animos demissa per aurem Quam quæ sunt oculi subjecta.*"
                                        Horace.

LONDON:
Printed by *Sampson Low, Marston, Searle, & Rivington,* of Crown Buildings, 188, *Fleet Street.* 1882.

Figure 128
Cover of *Beautiful Houses*.

Mrs Panton was one of the most popular authors of the 1880s and 1890s in the field of home decoration. She wrote 23 books, including some novels, notably *Nooks and Corners*, 1889, *Homes of Taste*, 1890, and *Suburban Residences and How to Circumvent Them*, 1896. Her most well-known work was *From Kitchen to Garrett, Hints to Young Householders*, 1887, which was in its eleventh edition ten years later:

> 'I have often been struck with amazement at discovering how few really practical guides there are that even profess to help newly married girls past those first shoals and quicksands that so often wreck the little vessel'.[29]

As in the case of other popular books on the home such as American Julia McNair Wright's *The Complete Home*, 1879, the text is made more accessible and readable as advice was given through imaginary situations involving fictitious characters, in this case, Edwin and Angelina.

It covered questions of house choosing and house management and furnishing 'from garrett to basement' (Figure 129), and covering topics such as servants, babies, and children's education.

> 'Penge and Dulwich are dreary and damp … the higher parts of Sydenham are to be preferred … those who do not mind the north side of London, Finchley, Bush Hill Park … and Enfield are all worthy of consideration'.[30]

It is clear that these books had a ready market; as Mrs Panton points out, 'very rich people can place themselves unreservedly in the hands of a professional decorator', an option not possible for her readers. This book was based on articles written by her in *The Lady's Pictorial* magazine, and for which she had 'thousands of correspondents'. She was a pioneer in this field:

> 'From my correspondence I have evolved quite a new profession, which I commend to any lady … I go to people's houses and advise them about their decorations, and tell them the best places to go for different things; I buy things for country ladies … we have now started a society for the employment of ladies who will either decorate a house entirely, make the chair-covers and curtains I recommend, or work at ladies' houses at dressmaking and upholstering'.[31]

Figure 129
Drawing-room scheme in *From Kitchen to Garrett*.

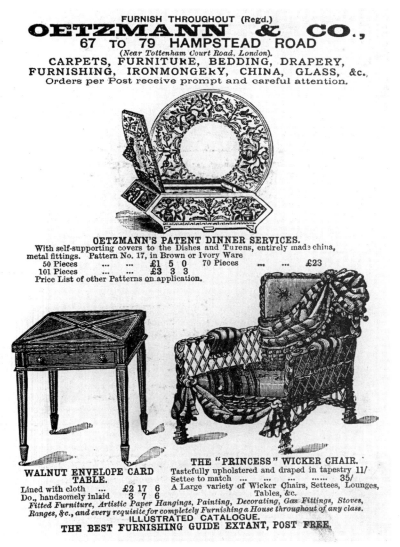

Figure 130
Oetzmann's advertisement in Mrs Panton's *Homes of Taste*.

Figure 131
Design for Vitremante window decoration which resembled stained glass.

Her books gave very specific advice on brandnames of goods and where to get them, for example, Smee, Treloar, and Maples. Amateur work, do-it-yourself, crochet, embroidery, etc., promoted by Mrs Panton and others, was a fashionable idea among the middle classes and prompted books entirely devoted to it, such as Beeton's *Ladies Bazaar and Fancy Fair Book*, c.1890s (Figure 131).

Publishers increasingly catered for a working-class market, with books such as Cassell's *Book of the Household*, 1897 edition, and Sylvia's *Home Help Series*. *The House and Its Furniture*, 1879, costing 1s, had an interesting section on definitions of six different types of dwellings from palace to cottage, for example, a 'villa' should 'stand in its own grounds, or … be accessible on three of its four sides … and will contain from ten to twenty rooms'; the book comments that the term villa is used 'indiscriminately' but that 'No house … should be called a villa … unless it has a good garden'.[32] Sylvia's *Book of Family Management*, published by a manufacturer, J.W. Shaw, Cheetham, Manchester, with 'Branches in every part of the Town', dealt with day-to-day subjects like cottage gardening and needlework, holiday excursions, maternity, infancy and childhood, washing day, cooking and furnishing. Cassell continued to produced economical multi-volumed sets after 1900. As mentioned in the Introduction, Gresham Publishing, an offshoot of Blackie & Son, published the six volumed *The Book of the Home*, 1909, whose author was Mrs Humphreys, or 'Madge' of *Truth*, as she was more popularly known.

REFERENCES

1 Michael Snodin and Maurice Howard, *Ornament; A Social History Since 1450*, Yale University Press in association with Victoria and Albert Museum, New Haven and London 1996, 30.

2 Ifor Edwards, *Decorative Cast Iron in Wales*, Gomer Press, Llandysul, 1989, 27.

3 Janet Myles, *L.N Cottingham 1787–1847*, Lund Humphries Publishers, London, 1996, 76.

4 see Robertson, E Graeme, and Joan Robertson, *Cast Iron Decoration*, Thames and Hudson, London, 1977, 1994, for examples.

5 *The Architectural Magazine*, 1834, 136.

6 *The Architectural Magazine*, 1834, 137.

7 Charlotte Gere, *The House Beautiful*, The Geffrye Museum, 2000, 35.

8 Thomas King, *Neo-Classical Furniture Designs, A Reprint of Thomas King's 'Modern Style of Cabinet Work Exemplified'*, Dover publications, New York, 1995, introduction by Thomas Gordon Smith, xi.

9 *Pictorial History of British Nineteenth Century Furniture Design*, Antique Collectors' Club, Suffolk, 1977, introduction by Edward Joy, xxviii.

10 B.J. Talbert, *Victorian Decorative Arts*, The American Life Foundation for The Athenium Library of Nineteenth Century America, New York, 1978, introduction, n.p.

11 B.J. Talbert, *Examples of Ancient and Modern Furniture*, 1876, in *Victorian Decorative Arts*, The American Life Foundation for The Athenium Library of Nineteenth Century America, New York, 1978, n.p.

12 Christopher Dresser, *Studies in Design*, Studio Editions, London, 1988, preface.

13 Eileen Harris, *British Architectural Books and Writers 1556–1785*, Cambridge University Press, 1990, 44.

14 Alfred Bartholomew, *Practical Specifications in Architecture*, 1840, preface.

15 David T. Yeomans, 'Early Carpenters' Manuals 1592–1820', *Journal of the Construction History Society,* volume 2, 1986, 28–9.

16 David T. Yeomans, 'Early Carpenters' Manuals 1592–1820', *Journal of the Construction History Society,* volume 2, 1986, 31.

17 *The Architectural Magazine*, volume 3, 1836, 226, 229.

18 Aileen, Reid, *Brentham; A History of the Pioneer Garden Suburb 1901–2001*, Brentham Heritage Society, London, 2000, 176.

19 *How to Keep House or Comfort and Elegance on £150–£200 a Year*, 6th ed 1832, 8–10.

20 Nancy Spain, *Mrs Beeton and her Husband*, Collins, London, 1948, 254.

21 J.H.Walsh, *A Manual of Domestic Economy*, Routledge, London, 1879 edition, 11.

22 J.H.Walsh, *A Manual of Domestic Economy*, Routledge, London, 1879 edition, 195–204.

23 John Gloag, *Mr Loudon's England*, Oriel Press Ltd, Newcastle, 1970, 61.

24 Asa Briggs, *Victorian Things*, Penguin Books, London, 1990, 215.

25 see introduction to Eastlake's *History of the Gothic Revival*, Leicester University Press, Leicester, 1970, by J. Mordaunt Crook, 15–19.

26 Mrs Loftie, *The Dining Room*, Macmillan, London, 1878, preface.

27 R.W. Edis, *The Decoration and Furniture of Town Houses*, EP Publishing Limited, 1972, x.

28 Mrs Haweis, *Beautiful Houses*, Sampson Low, London, 1882, 13–14.

29 Mrs J.E. Panton, *From Kitchen to Garrett*, Ward & Downey, London, 1888, 1.

30 Mrs J.E. Panton, *From Kitchen to Garrett*, Ward & Downey, London, 1888, 3.

31 Mrs J.E. Panton, *From Kitchen to Garrett*, Ward & Downey, London, 1888, preface.

32 *The House and Its Furniture*, 1879, 2–3.

4   Trade catalogues and journals

TRADE CATALOGUES

The Victorian period is very much the age of the trade catalogue and the building journal. Over the course of the nineteenth century we see an increase in
their importance, particularly in the final quarter of the century, and by 1900
these types of publications had overtaken some conventional modes of transmitting information. Such a shift reflected vast changes occurring in the building industry in response to the demand for housing and ornamentation
generally. Journals provided the same type of information as books, patterns,
prices, and instruction, but also trade news and correspondence and information was regularly updated. Firms increasingly advertised their wares in journals,
and indeed in manuals and price books, made easier after tax on advertising
was dropped in 1853. In their effort to compete in supplying the building trades
with ready-made materials and components, firms developed a large appara-
tus of publicity, including extensive and profusely illustrated catalogues. This
was made possible by cheap printing methods and new modes of illustration,
and large companies issued various catalogues for different markets.

The modern trade catalogue, with numbered and priced patterns,[1] developed in the mid-eighteenth century from traditional forms of communication
and selling, for example, ornamental prints of designs,[2] and pattern and button
cards (which enclosed samples of the product for sale) in response to the
increasing need to find more efficient ways of selling products in a fast changing world. Early catalogues of books, maps and globes, scientific instruments
and flowers and plants are among the trade catalogue's predecessors, and
notably, Thomas Chippendale's *The Gentleman's and Cabinet Maker's Director* of 1754, with designs which could be bought from the factory.[3] The tools
trade, notably John Wyke of Liverpool, and brass and cutlery manufacturers
of the Midlands and the North, began to issue trade catalogues between the
late 1750s and 1770s.[4] Catalogues were expensive to produce, because of
copperplate engraving and prices had to be added in by hand afterwards. Some
firms used pattern cards and trade catalogues concurrently to begin with, for
example, Wedgewood.[5] Designs were often drawn lifesize in early catalogues,
a hangover from using actual samples.[6]

An early trade catalogue for the building trades was that of Mrs Eleanor
Coade's firm of 1784, which contained 700 designs in the artificial stone,
including fire surrounds and internal and external paterae. A doorway might
cost £5, or if this could not be afforded, a small Lion keystone 6 inches high
cost 2s.[7] As one of the few women in business in this period, she was well

Figure 132
Coade etching of doorway, used in Bedford Square, London. Similar designs were used all over this area of London, for example, Harley Street and Baker Street. (Courtesy of the Trustees of Sir John Soane's Museum.)

known and Coadestone was used by major and minor architects of the time for example, Adam, Nash, Soane, Crunden, Nicholson and Papworth, on houses all over Britain, and its influence spread far beyond (Figure 132). Fanlights, in addition to designs in pattern books of designs, were obtainable from trade catalogues such as that of Underwood and Doyle of c.1813.

The use of the trade catalogue was common by the early nineteenth century, and by the Great Exhibition of 1851, all exhibitors had trade catalogues to give to visitors. In 1836, Charles Frederick Bielefeld produced a trade catalogue of papier mâché designs. *Ornaments in every style of design, practically applicable to the decoration of the interiors of domestic and public buildings and intended for the assistance of the architect, builder, upholsterer and decorator*, enlarged in 1850, contained numerous designs for roses, cornices and console brackets, and sought to fulfil the increasing demand for materials which could instantly indicate the style intended for an interior (Figure 133). Although this is a trade catalogue with pages of designs and prices, it combined advertising the product, with a historical overview of 'the particular circumstances which gave rise to the adoption of

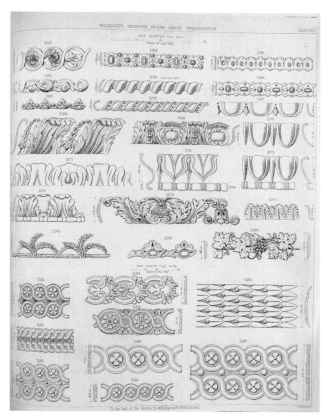

Figure 133
Plate from the 1850 edition of Bielefeld's catalogue, with prices ranging from 3d per foot for 1174 'antique' to 10d for 1159 'rose, thistle and shamrock' designs. (Courtesy of V & A Picture Library.)

papier mâché by the architectural decorator in England'. He traced how Elizabethan and classic styles brought in bold plasterwork and produced a need for 'contrivances', that is papier mâché from France and how the large trade in papier mâché in the eighteenth century was held back by imperfect technology. Given the stylistic eclecticism of the early nineteenth century, plaster was 'totally inapplicable to the exact imitation of the bold florid carvings … while to carve in wood … would occasion a cost far beyond the means of all ordinary purses.' Technological improvements resulted in a tough, rapidly manufactured, cheap product, easily assembled using screws. Bielefeld said:

> 'Nothing can possibly be so convenient as papier mâché … many hundreds of flowers or paterae are annually sent from the manufactory to be fixed upon ceilings of the smaller class of private dwellings, the erection of which the increasing population of the country is requiring in almost every town in the kingdom. These are sometimes merely used to give a neat finish to the appearance of the room.'[8]

The look of the trade catalogue altered and costs dropped with the arrival of the steam press and the move to wood engraving from the 1830s. Chromolithography also began to be used and was to become increasingly important; Mintons was an early user, producing a full-colour catalogue in the early 1860s; their 1885 catalogue was an early example of photographic reproduction of designs where moulded surfaces need to be shown.

The pattern books of cast iron designs by L.N. Cottingham and Henry Shaw of the 1820s and 1830s mentioned earlier, were superseded after mid century

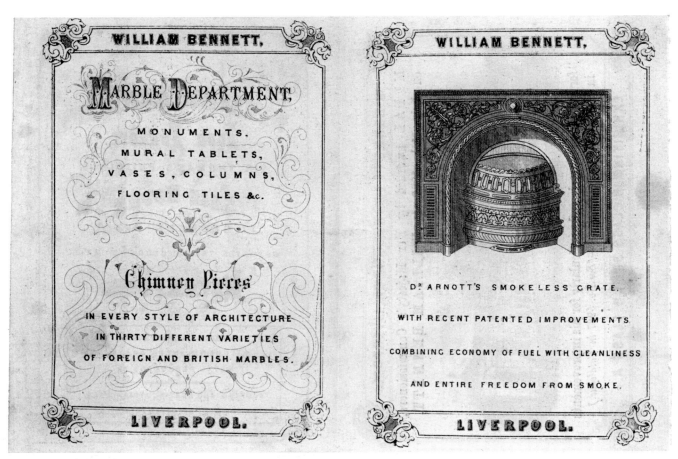

Figure 134
George Bennett, Liverpool, catalogue c.1862 shows firegrates, ranges, garden furniture and tools and a full-page illustration of their premises, together with notice of their medal at the 1862 Exhibition.

by the trade catalogues of iron firms,[9] such as Coalbrookedale Company of Shropshire, and Glasgow foundries Walter Macfarlane & Co, George Smith & Co and MacDowall, Steven & Co., and Carron Company of Falkirk, whose designs appear all over Britain and abroad. Many trade catalogues harked back to Cottingham and Shaw forms[10] and pirating of designs was a problem, despite copyright protection.

Iron catalogues of the 1870s became more substantial; Coalbrookedale Co catalogue of 1875 had 12 sections of wares, 572 pages, 11 × 13 inches and weighed 10 lb. Walter Macfarlane's catalogue of 1882, appeared in a full-size colour version, and also a black-and-white pocket-sized version (Figures 135–137). The inconsistent numbering and non-dating typical of many catalogues, goes back to practices of early trade catalogues – old and new designs were used in the same catalogue and pages kept in loose sheets for re-compiling to suit needs at a later date. Prices could be listed separately for the same reason. As happened in building journals, the use of the latest illustrative techniques, such as photolithography, was a matter of pride and giving the catalogue a 'cutting edge' flavour.

The progressive Norwich iron firm of Barnard, Bishop and Barnard also produced catalogues around the same time, with designs for firegrates, garden furniture and other goods. Barnards were well known for their innovative grates, both in a technological and artistic sense, and they were frequently highlighted

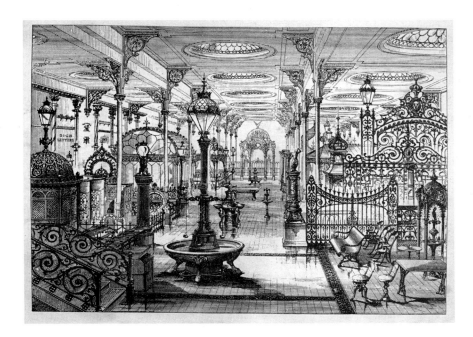

Figure 135
Walter Macfarlane and Co's premises, 1882.

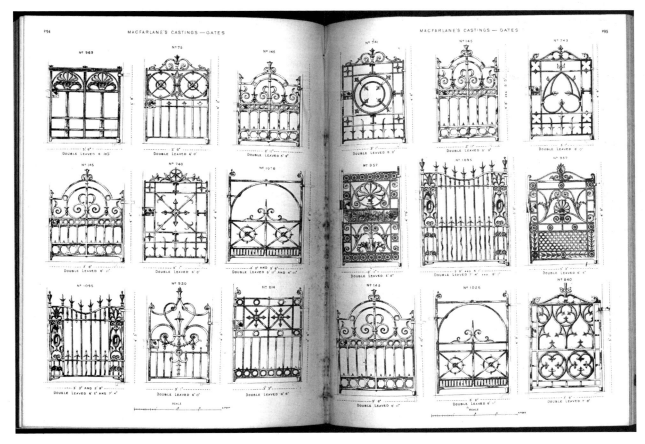

Figure 136
Macfarlane's designs for gates, 1882.

MACFARLANE'S CASTINGS — BALCONIES

Figure 137
Macfarlane's balcony designs, 1882.

in the building journals of the later nineteenth century. Just as the Adam brothers had been associated with Carron Company a century earlier, Barnards used tiles in their designs designed by a range of artists such as Kate Greenaway, William Morris and William De Morgan.[11]

If a Barnard, Bishop and Barnard grate, with its Oriental-style birds and flora, was desirable in a fashionable Aesthetic interior, terracotta and moulded brick were essential ingredients for the exterior of a fashionable Queen Anne house. Blanchard & Company and John Blashfield, both of which companies had early links with Coade, and Doulton & Company, were early important companies in the field. Doulton began making terracotta in the 1820s and by the 1880s their catalogues were full of a wide range of building requisites. The influence of terracotta catalogues appears as elaborate decoration on villas in towns with terracotta companies nearby, for example, Hathern Station Brick and Terracotta Company of Loughborough. The most popular products would have been items such as finials and gate posts which did not have to course in with brickwork.[12] The Enfield Brick and Tile and Terracotta Company, Accrington, a major brick area, produced a small catalogue of their products in 1891, all illustrations done in green litho ink (Figures 138 and 139). This trade catalogue was clearly well used and has a design for a gatepost cut out.

Another small paperback catalogue of The Cheap Wood Company of 1900 shows how far selling joinery items had come since the early days of the timber business. In Jewson's case, this involved looking for business in Diss or Beccles on market day, and if none was forthcoming, seeking out local builders and riding back to Norwich late in the evening (Figures 140–142).[13]

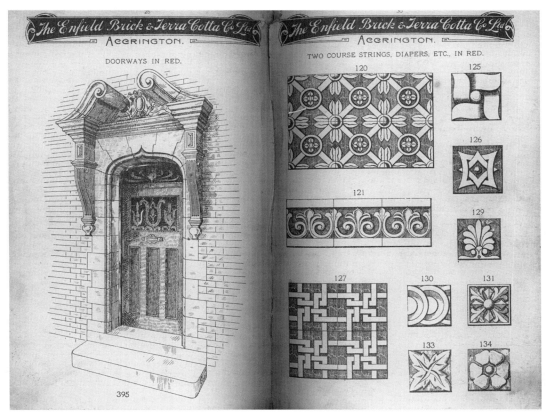

Figure 138
Doorway and string courses.

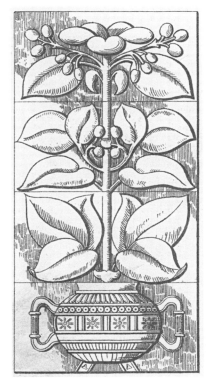

Figure 139
Swags and panels.

Figure 140
Paperback cover.

Figure 141
Choice of turned balluster designs.

PORCHES.

This drawing represents a Porch specially designed by the **Cheap Wood Company**. It is of substantial construction, and well finished. The design is an unique one, and is readily adapted to almost any style of architecture.

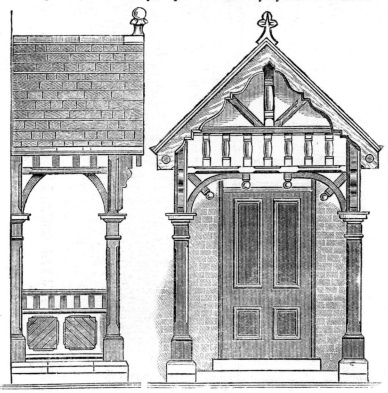

SPECIFICATION.

Size—9 ft. high × 6 ft. wide × 4 ft. deep.
Front Posts out of 5 × 5.
Back Posts out of 5 × 4.
Rails out of   ...   4 × 3.
Panels framed and fitted with diagonal **V**-jointed matching.
Roof fitted with matching and oak shingles.
The whole complete and ready for fixing for the sum of £11 10s.

Quotations given for any description of Porches on receipt of full Particulars.

Figure 142
Design for a porch.

While one tendency in trade catalogue production was towards cheaply produced paperbacks, the late nineteenth century also saw increasingly lavish catalogues from large manufacturers, which became a key source of design ideas for the building trades. Builders merchants grew in number from 100 in 1870 to 1300 by 1910.[14] Catalogues could contain samples of the product, for example, paint, and views of premises and facilities, along with detailed delivery schedules and prices. The large general builders merchant of Young and Marten Ltd, Stratford, London, founded 1872, is an excellent example of a firm who produced a range of catalogues for the various trades and sometimes different markets with a trade, and made great use of the range of illustrative techniques, in particular chromolithography (Figure 143). Their 1898 catalogue demonstrates the wide range of designs within any one type of product, resulting from mass production and standardization (Figures 144–146).

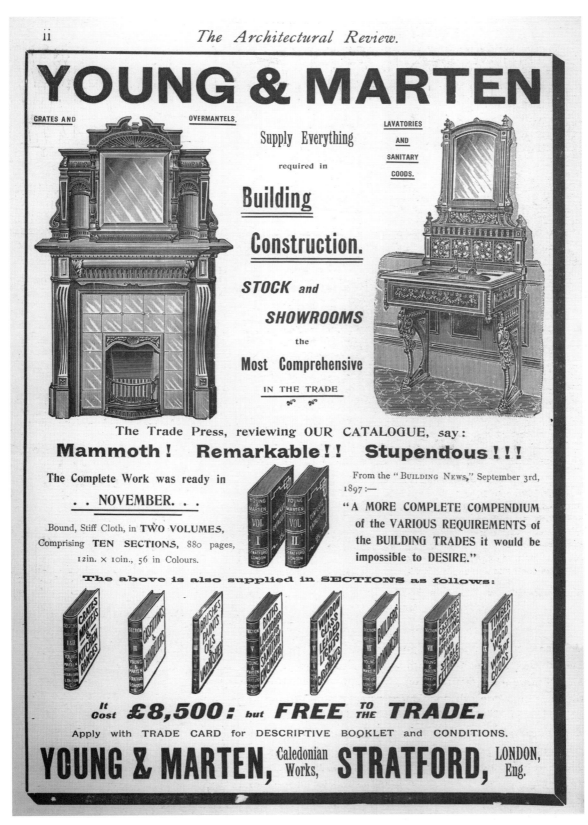

Figure 143
Advertisement for Young & Marten's catalogues, 1897. Their 1905 catalogue has six books of paperhangings, from one containing 'the cheapest class of Paperhangings suitable for cottages' to that of 'best class' hangings, including best Sanitaries, Satinettes and Tapestries, chosen from the leading British and Continental manufacturers' selections.

Figure 144
Young and Marten floor tiles.

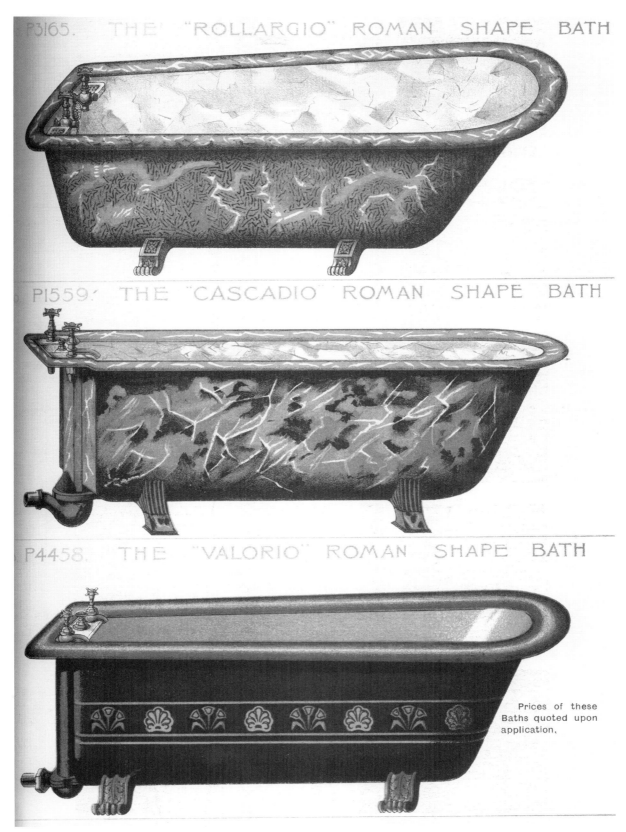

P3165. THE "ROLLARGIO" ROMAN SHAPE BATH

P1559. THE "CASCADIO" ROMAN SHAPE BATH

P4458. THE "VALORIO" ROMAN SHAPE BATH

Prices of these Baths quoted upon application,

Figure 145
Choice of baths in Young and Marten's catalogue.

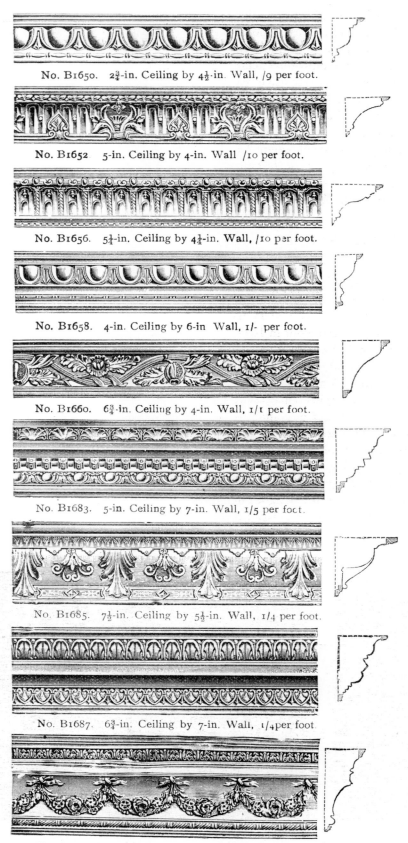

No. B1650. $2\frac{3}{4}$-in. Ceiling by $4\frac{1}{2}$-in. Wall, /9 per foot.

No. B1652.   5-in. Ceiling by 4-in. Wall /10 per foot.

No. B1656. $5\frac{1}{4}$-in. Ceiling by $4\frac{1}{4}$-in. Wall, /10 per foot.

No. B1658.   4-in. Ceiling by 6-in Wall, 1/- per foot.

No. B1660. $6\frac{3}{4}$-in. Ceiling by 4-in. Wall, 1/1 per foot.

No. B1683.   5-in. Ceiling by 7-in. Wall, 1/5 per foot.

No. B1685. $7\frac{1}{2}$-in. Ceiling by $5\frac{1}{2}$-in. Wall, 1/4 per foot.

No. B1687. $6\frac{3}{4}$-in. Ceiling by 7-in. Wall, 1/4 per foot.

No. B1689. $5\frac{1}{4}$-in. Ceiling by $10\frac{3}{4}$-in. Wall, 1/5 per foot.

Figure 146
Examples of Young & Marten's cornice designs.

The elaborate trade catalogue caught on hugely with furnishing firms, for example Hamptons' substantial catalogue of 1894, with its colour illustrations, 50 collotypes and 2000 halftone blocks photographed from the stock, showing every aspect of the home, from complete interior schemes to individual items like fireguards and lighting fixtures. This catalogue demonstrated the perceived suitability of certain styles for particular rooms of the house at this time, such as Elizabethan for the dining room and Georgian for the drawing room.[15]

Finally, an interesting turn occurs with the trade catalogue of Boulton and Paul, is an iron company in Norwich, where their building catalogue of designs for small houses of 1909, such as a 'weekend cottage for a motorist', takes on the form of an architectural pattern book and is entitled *Bungalows and Cottage Residences, An Architectural Treatise on Country Houses, Their Design and Equipment*.

JOURNALS OF ARCHITECTURE, BUILDING TRADES AND HOME FURNISHING

The origins of magazine publishing lie in pamphlets, broadsides, ballads, chapbooks and almanacs. The first magazine to be produced was in Germany in 1663, while the first to be published in Britain was the *Athenian Gazette* in 1690. The first women's magazine, *The Ladies' Mercury*, came out in 1693. Typical of Georgian and Regency period was *Lady's Monthly Museum*, 1798–1806, and 1817–28. Its rival, *Ackermann's Repository of the Arts*, 1809–28, was at the forefront of taste and technical innovation, using the new medium of lithography from 1817. Originally intended as a general magazine, in its final 12 years it specifically aimed at women. The magazine contained fabric samples, hand-coloured plates of dress fashions, designs for country houses, garden buildings and furniture, and illustrations of the interiors of Wedgewood's showrooms and Ackermann's Repository (Figure 147). Groups of plates were later published in book form, as in A.C. Pugin's *Gothic Furniture*, 1827. The classical style was much illustrated for furniture designs but in 1817 there was the first recorded illustration of the new interest in Elizabethan style, followed by Egyptian in 1825–7.

Figure 147
Design for a fountain in *Ackermann's Repository of the Arts* in 1819.

While most of the early general magazines were high quality and aimed at the leisured classes, cheaper ones began to appear from the 1830s, with an increasing moral tone and emphasis on self-improvement, for example, Cassell's *Workingman's Friend and Family Instructor*, 1850. As domesticity became the ideal for women to aspire to, so women's magazines became home centred in content and moral in tone, for example, *The Ladies Treasury*, 1857.

The first woman's journal to deal with the subject of home management and give practical instruction, was Samuel Beeton's *The Englishwoman's Domestic Magazine*, 1852, costing 2d. Better-class women's magazines became an increasingly important source of ideas and advice on interior decoration and, as we have seen, their columnists often later turned their advice into book form. Cheap titles for the working classes multiplied in the final decade of the century, with the formation of many more publishing houses, notably Harmsworth and Pearson, responsible for *Home Notes* and *Home Chat*, founded in 1894 and 1895, respectively; costing 1d, with fiction and practical articles on nutrition, hygiene, and childcare, these paralleled the trend which has been seen in home manuals.[16]

Journals were a crucial means of transmitting architectural ideas, and they gained in importance over books in this respect during the Victorian period. The

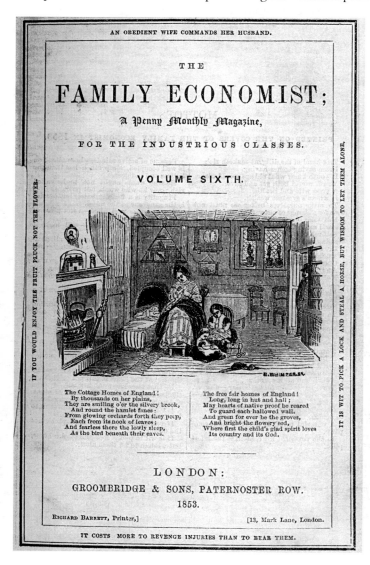

Figure 148

The Family Economist, 1853, covered a range of subjects, including house painting and furniture.

first journal in Britain or the USA dedicated to architecture and building was *The Architectural Magazine and Journal of Improvement in Architecture, Building and Furnishing and in the various arts and trades connected therewith*, by J.C. Loudon, 1834–8. The eighteenth century had seen the appearance of Edward Oakley's *The Magazine of Architecture, Perspective and Sculpture*, 1733, and *The Builders Magazine*, 1774, neither of which were actually journals; the latter, for instance, comprised a builder's dictionary, a description of rates of housing according to Act of Parliament and a collection of patterns for various buildings, with plate descriptions, and was published in parts, as was common practice, *The Architectural Magazine* was a monthly periodical, based on Loudon's book *The Encyclopaedia of Cottage, Farm and Villa Architecture* published the preceding year. The subject matter was broad, from articles about transparent blinds and Mr Austin's artificial stone, to book reviews of major works by Pugin and a series of articles by John Ruski,n and domestic architecture in particular was given a high profile.

Following the closure of Loudon's magazine in 1838, in late 1842 Joseph Aloysius Hansom, architect and inventor of the Hansom cab, founded *The Builder* magazine. It was advertised as 'an illustrated weekly magazine for the drawing room, the studio, the office, the workshop and the cottage'. It became arguably the most important journal of the century, with a wide readership among the developing professions and new trades such as sanitary engineers. George Godwin was its editor from 1844 to 1883, and his interests in social issues, such as slum overcrowding, shaped the character of the *The Builder*. Competing journals in the field of architecture and building followed the formation of *The Builder*; *The Building News*, in 1855, *The Architect*, in 1869, and *British Architect*, in 1874, and *Building World* and *The Architectural Review*, both in 1895. *The Building News* of the 1850s and 1860s featured issues of style and technology, for example,

DESIGN FOR A CONCRETE HOUSE FOR MR LASCELLES.
DESIGNED BY ERNEST NEWTON, ARCHITECT.

Figure 149
Ernest Newton's design for a concrete house for Mr Lascelles, *The Building News*, 1881.

materials and styles for the firesurround, and the search for solutions to the problems of domestic heating; the issues of the 1870s had much on house decoration and practical articles on plumbing and damp prevention, for example, publicity given to the invention of a revolutionary firegrate design by Barnard, Bishop and Barnard of Norwich in the early 1880s. This firm's work, as mentioned, was regarded as technologically and artistically avant garde, and so fitted the progressive outlook of the paper, owned by Passmore Edwards, who was known for his radical views. The avant-garde designer E.W. Godwin, was involved with the paper's production, likewise Maurice B. Adams, in whose hands the architects of the Queen Anne style, for example Shaw, enjoyed considerable support. The journal featured a sketching club, regular competitions to design small-scale works such as a boathouse or item of furniture, and themes such as designs for artists' houses by leading architects (Figures 149–152).

In 1877, *The Illustrated Carpenter and Builder* was established, a weekly magazine, for joiners, decorators, painters, plumbers, gas fitters, architects, etc., price 1d, edited by John Black (Figure 154). *The Illustrated Carpenter and Builder* was a response to the sudden changes in the housebuilding picture,[17] with the arrival on the scene of the artisan builder, a product of the 1860s, and the accompanying boom in lower middle-class villa building from the late

THE BUILDING NEWS, JUN. 25 1880

Figure 150
J. J. Stevenson's design for an artist's house, 1880.

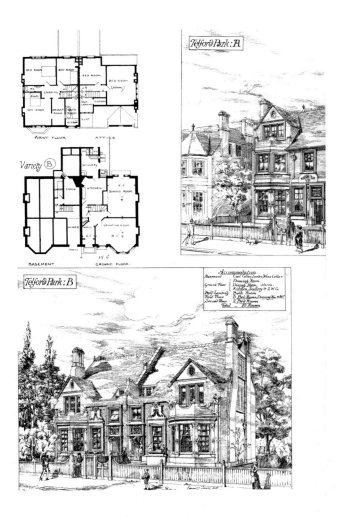

Figure 151
Smaller houses in Telford Park, built along Bedford
Park lines by Edward J. Tarver, 1880.

The · SHAKSPERE · DINING-ROOM · SET · BY E.W.GODWIN F.S.A   MADE BY WILLIAM WATT · OCT 81

Figure 152
The 'Shakspere' dining room set by E.W. Godwin, made by William Watt, 1881.

1870s to 1890s. It was a lower class of paper than *The Building News*, both in quality of production and in content, more practical in tone with trade information and the advertisements were for practical products on the whole, such as tools, builders supplies and so on. There were some attempts to deal with the current fashions, illustrating for example, a Queen Anne window fitment (Figure 154) or a modern vernacular style semi-detached house design. The designs for small detached, semi-detached and terraced houses, illustrated were generally small scale as opposed to full-page *Building News* style, and tended to be conservative in taste, frequently degraded versions of Classic or Gothic in style, but nonetheless useful to the small builder (Figures 156–158); in the preface of the 1894 volume, the editor noted that the magazine had survived strong competition from the new building magazines on the market.

While the architectural and building magazines occasionally illustrated designs for wallpapers, furniture, etc., it should be briefly mentioned that magazines specifically on furniture and furnishings came out in the latter part

Figure 153
Advertisement for the magazine in 1897.

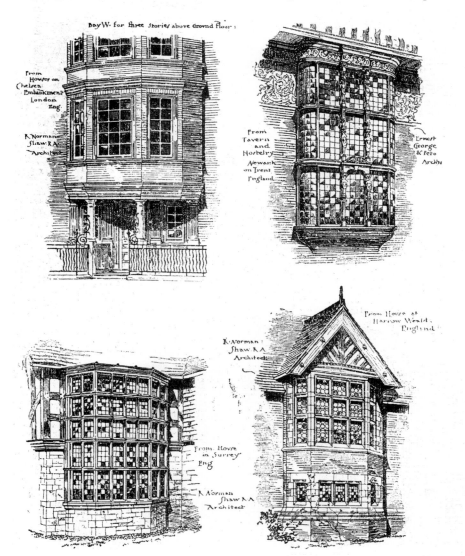

Figure 154
Fashionable windows by R.N. Shaw and others in *The Illustrated Carpenter and Builder*, 1882.

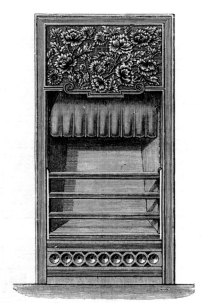

BARNARD, BISHOP, AND BARNARD'S "GLOW" COMBUSTION STOVE.

Figure 155
The fashionable Barnard, Bishop and Barnard grate, 1881.

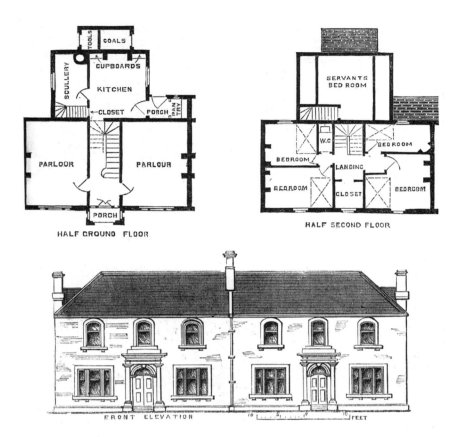

Figure 156
Designs for small houses, 1882.

Figure 157
Villa design, 1882.

Figure 158
Designs for semi-detached houses, 1894.

of the century. such as *Furniture Gazette*, 1872, and *The Cabinet Maker and Art Furnisher, Treating of Furniture, Upholstery, Decoration, Textile Fabrics, Art Metal Work, Timber and Woodworking Machinery*, 1875, taking on the role of the pattern book of earlier in the century (Figures 160–163). The journal compiled a book, available free to businesses, listing hundreds of buyers of cabinet goods and furnishing materials compiled from readers' testimonials, so that 'advertisers will see … that their advertisements really reach the leading buyers'. After 1900 these journals reflect a new trend; principles of simplicity, naturalness, honesty, good decent solid workmanship of handmade objects, championed by Ruskin, had formed the basis of the new artistic ideals of William Morris and the new Arts and Crafts movement, and its wider exposure at the Arts and Crafts exhibitions from 1888.

Catering for other specific branches of the trades were journals such as *The House Decorator and School of Design*, founded 1880, price 1d, aimed at painters, plumbers, gas fitters, brass and wire workers, builders, carpenters and cabinet-makers, and *The Plumber and Decorator* and *Journal of Heating, Ventilating, Gas and Sanitary Engineering*, started two years earlier. Builders merchants had their own magazine from 1897, *The Builders Merchant* which included *The Quarry*, costing 7s per year. Ernest Benn had great success in the field of technical and trade journals, turning around the fortunes of the *Hardware Trade Journal* sold to Benn, and buying a small rival paper, *Ironmongery*. Other specialist journals in this field included *The Ironmonger and Metal Trades Advertiser* was established in 1859, as a weekly magazine costing 6d. In the early 1880s, it was a cheaply produced paper, comprising largely world iron trade news and many advertisements of all kinds, from lawnmowers and light fixtures, to heavy engineering and machine tools. Exporting and the Empire were prominent themes among the advertisements (Figures 164 and 165).

Figure 159
Designs for freizes and cornices, 1878 in *The Illustrated Carpenter and Builder*.

Figure 160
Previously a commercial traveller for a furniture company, J. Williams Benn founded *The Cabinet Maker* in 1875, to advocate better design and production of furniture. His eldest son, Ernest Benn, left school at 15 and started work on his father's paper, first as an office boy, then as a traveller, selling advertising space, and finally as the manager of *The Cabinet Maker*.

Figure 161
An inexpensive dining room in the Renaissance style in *The Cabinet Maker* 1885–6. Styles of furniture for the year, also included Queen Anne, Louis Seize, Century Guild, Jacobean, eighteenth century, Tudor and Sheraton.

MOORISH FURNITURE,
made in Cairo.

Imported by
MESSRS. ROTTMANN, STROME & CO.

Figure 162 Moorish furniture, made in Cairo, Messrs Rottmann, Strome & Co in *The Cabinet Maker* 1885–6. Japanese designs for total room schemes, cosy corners and individual items were also very regularly illustrated.

Figure 163
Schemes for curtain arrangements in *The Cabinet Maker*, 1885–6.

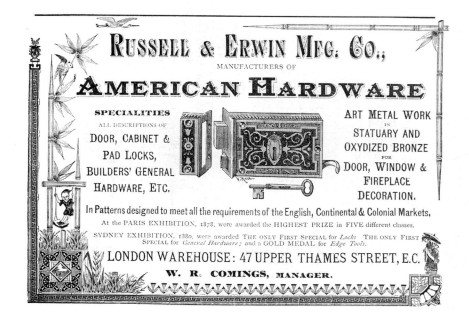

Figure 164
Advertisement in *The Ironmonger and Metal Trades Advertiser*, 1881.

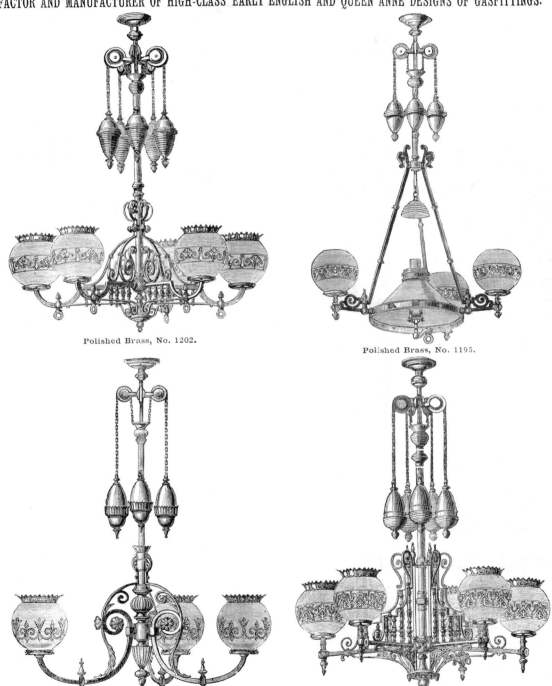

Figure 165
Advertisement in *The Ironmonger and Metal Trades Advertiser*, 1881.

REFERENCES

1 Theodore, R., Crom, *Trade catalogues 1542–1842*, Melrose, Florida, 1989, 2.

2 Michael Snodin and Maurice Howard, *Ornament; A Social History Since 1450*, Yale University Press in association with Victoria and Albert Museum, New Haven and London 1996, 54.

3 National Art Library Internet site, *Trade Catalogues*.

4 Theodore, R. Crom, *Trade catalogues 1542–1842*, Melrose, Florida, 1989, 4.

5 Theodore, R. Crom, *Trade catalogues 1542–1842*, Melrose, Florida, 1989, 41.

6 Philip Walker, *The Victorian Catalogue of Tools for Trades and Crafts*, Studio Editions, London, 1994, n.p.

7 Alison Kelly, *Mrs Coade's Stone*, The Self Publishing Association Ltd, Upton-on-Severn, Worcs, in conjunction with The Georgian Group, 1990, 160.

8 C.F.Bielefeld, *Ornaments in every style of design, practically applicable to the decoration of the interiors of domestic and public buildings and intended for the assistance of the architect, builder, upholdsterer and decorator,* 1850 edition, preface.

9 E Graeme Robertson and Joan Robertson, *Cast Iron Decoration*, Thames and Hudson, London, 1977, 1994. 21.

10 Ifor Edwards, *Decorative Cast Iron in Wales*, Gomer Press, Llandysul, 1989, 32.

11 Jon Catleugh, *William De Morgan Tiles*, Richard Dennis, Ilminster, 1991, 32.

12 Michael Stratton, *The Terracotta Revival*, Victor Gollancz, London, 1993, 98.

13 C.B.Jewson, ed., *Typescript-JWJ 1816–1882*, privately published, 1948 (located in Norwich Record Office).

14 Stefan Muthesius, *The English Terraced House*, Yale University Press, New Haven and London, 1982, 30.

15 *The Victorian Catalogue of Household Furnishing*, introduced by Stephen Calloway, Studio Editions, London 1994.

16 see Cynthia L. White, *Women's Magazines, 1693–1986,* Joseph, London, 1970.

17 John Summerson, *The Unromantic Castle*, Thames and Hudson, London, 1990, 232.

5   Postscript

In April 1893 a new magazine, *The Studio*, was launched, aimed at the huge middle-class audience. It became the most important art and design magazine of the late nineteenth century, as *The Art Journal* had been in previous years. Edited by Gleeson White, a prominent feature of the magazine was its international dimension and readership. *The Studio* covered a wide scope across design, architecture and fine art, featuring articles by, or about, avant-garde designers, such as William Morris, C.A. Voysey, M.H. Baillie Scott, and Lasenby Liberty. It continued to play a key role in the transmission of taste into the twentieth century. Magazines such as this added to the flood of publications on house design and interior decoration; at the top of the range were books featuring the work of important designers, such as W. Shaw Sparrow's *The British Home of Today*, 1904, and books by Muthesius, Baillie Scott, Weaver, and others, profusely illustrated in the new medium of photographic reproduction. At the cheap end of the market were books such as the paperback Arthur S. Jennings' *The Home Beautiful, a Practical Guide to the Artistic Decoration and Furnishing of Moderate Sized Houses on Inexpensive Lines*, 1908, costing 6d. This little book was specifically not intended for wealthy homeowners; with sections on 'Difficulties of Harmonising Old Furniture with New Decoration', 'Morris and his influence', 'Non-poisonous paints', and 'Venetian Blinds', it creates a vivid impression of the needs and priorities of the ordinary house-holder. Advertisements for products such as Hall's Sanitary Washable Distemper, Ripolin Paint, Flooryline dark oak floor varnish, and Oetzmann's bungalow-cottages, costing £200–£230, and furnished for 45 guineas, add to this picture. Sources such as these demonstrate the nature of the need and desire for advice and ideas among the housebuilding industry and the public by the Edwardian period.

Concentrating on publications rather than the actual houses has been the focus of this book, and this approach allows us to view Victorian houses from a particular angle; through the modes of depicting buildings and the words of the authors, we can see very directly how contemporaries regarded the business of designing and building houses and what their priorities were, and the legacy of their publications is still with us today in the built forms which make such a major contribution to our towns and cities. The significance of their task of transmitting ideas about house design and decoration is apparent in the sense of commitment and pride demonstrated in all of these types of publications; as M.H. Baillie Scott said in *Houses and Gardens*, published in 1906:

> 'For the building and adornment of the house is surely the most important as well as the most human expression of the Art of man'.

Bibliography

Abbey, John Roland, *Life in England In Aquatint and Lithography, 1770–1860*, Maggs, 1953.

Agius, Pauline Agius, *British Furniture 1880–1915*, Antique Collectors' Club, Suffolk, n.d.

Aldrich, Megan, *Gothic Revival*, Phaidon Press Ltd, London, 1994.

Allen, C.B., *Cottage Building Hints for Improving the Dwellings of the Working Classes and the Poor*, Lockwood, London, 1849–50, 10th ed 1886.

Antique Collectors Club, *The Birth of The Studio 1893–5*, Suffolk, n.d., introduction by Simon Houfe.

Archer, John, *The Literature of British Domestic Architecture 1715–1842*, The MIT Press, Cambridge, Mass. and London, 1985.

Arrowsmith, H.W and Arrowsmith, A., *The House Decorator and Painter's Guide*, Kelly, London, 1840.

Aslin, Elizabeth, *The Aesthetic Movement*, Ferndale, London, 1981.

Atterbury, Paul and Wainwright, Clive, eds, *Pugin: A Gothic Passion*, Yale University Press, New Haven and London, in association with The Victoria and Albert Museum, 1994.

Audsley, W.J. and Audsley, G.A., *Cottage, Lodge and Villa Architecture*, Mackenzie, London, Edinburgh and Glasgow, 1869.

Ayres, James, *The Shell Book of the Home in Britain*, Faber and Faber, London, 1981.

Ayres, James, *Building the Georgian City*, Paul Mellon Centre, Yale University Press, New Haven and London, 1998.

Beard, Geoffrey, *Craftsmen and Interior Decoration in England, 1660–1820*, Bloomsbury Books, London, 1981.

Beeton, Mrs Isabella, *Book of Household Management*, Ward Lock, London, 1861.

Berg, Maxine, *The Age of Manufactures 1700–1820*, Routledge, London, 2nd edition 1994.

Blackburne, E.L., *Suburban and Rural Architecture*, Hagger, London, 1867.

Blackie, *Villa and Cottage Architecture*, Blackie, London and Glasgow, 1868.

Blackie, Agnes A.C., *Blackie and Son 1809–1959*, Blackie and Son Ltd, London and Glasgow.

Blutman, Sandra, 'Books of Designs for Country Houses, 1780–1815', *Architectural History*, 11, 1968, 25–33.

Bridson, Gavin and Wakeman, Geoffrey, *Printmaking and Picture Printing*, The Plough Press, Oxford and The Bookpress Ltd, Williamsburg, Virginia, 1984.

Booth, Charles, *Life and Labour of the People in London*, Macmillan, London,1895.

Brand, Ken, *The Park Estate, Nottingham*, Nottingham Civic Society, n.d.

Briggs, Asa, *Victorian Things*, Penguin Books, London, 1990.

Bristow, Ian, *Architectural Colour in British Interiors 1615–1840*, Paul Mellon Centre, Yale University Press, 1996.

Bristow, Ian, *Interior House-Painting Colours and Technology 1615–1840*, Paul Mellon centre, Yale University Press, 1996.

Brodie, A., Felstead, J., Franklin, J. and Pinfield, L., *Directory of British Architects 1834–1914*, 1996.

Brookes, S.H., *Designs for Cottage and Villa Architecture*, Kelly, London, 1839.

Burnett, John, *A Social History of Housing 1815–1970*, Methuen and Co Ltd, London, 1980.

Cassell's Household Guide, 1869-71.

Caffyn, Lucy, *Workers' Housing in West Yorkshire, 1750–1920*, Royal Commission on Historic Monuments of England, HMSO, 1986.

Calloway, S., ed., *The Elements of Style*, Mitchell Beazley, London, 1991.

Catleugh, Jon, *William De Morgan Tiles*, Richard Dennis, Ilminster, 1991.

Chafer, Denise, *The Arts Applied*, B. Weinreb Architectural Books Ltd, 1975.

Clarke, Linda, *Building Capitalism*, Routledge, London, 1992.

Colvin, Howard, *A Biographical Dictionary of British Architects, 1600–1840*, Paul Mellon Centre, Yale University Press, New Haven and London, 3rd edition, 1995.

Cornforth, John, *English Interiors, 1700–1848*, Barrie and Jenkins, 1978.

Cottingham, L.N., *The Ornamental Metal Worker's Director*, 1824.

Christie, Christopher, *The British Country House in the Eighteenth Century*, Manchester University Press, 2000.

Crom, Theodore, R., *Trade Catalogues 1542–1842*, Melrose, Florida, 1989.

Cruikshank, Dan and Peter Wyld, *Georgian Town Houses and their Details*, Butterworth Architecture, revised and reprinted edition, 1990.

Curwen, Harold, *Processes of Graphic Reproduction in Printing*, Faber and Faber, London, 1947.

Darley, Gillian, *Villages of Vision*, The Architectural Press Ltd, London 1975.

Davidoff, Leonore and Hall, Catherine, *Family Fortunes: Men and Women of the English Middle Class 1780–1850*, Hutchinson, London, 1987.

Dixon, Roger. and Muthesius, Stefan, *Victorian Architecture*, Thames and Hudson, London, 1978.

Dobson, E., *A Rudimentary Treatise on the Manufacture of Bricks and Tiles*, Virtue, London, 4th edition 1868.

Donner, Peter F.R. (pseud. for Nikolaus Pevsner), 'The End of the Pattern Books', *Architectural Review ,*XCIII:555, March 1943, 75-79.

Downing, Andrew Jackson, *Cottage Residences*, 1842, reprinted by Dover Publications, New York, 1981.

Downing, Andrew Jackson, *The Architecture of Country Houses*, 1850, reprinted by Dover Publications, New York, 1969.

Dresser, Christopher, *Studies in Design*, Studio Editions, London, 1988, introduction by Stephen Calloway.

Dyos, H.J., *Victorian Suburb: A Study of the Growth of Camberwell*, Leicester University Press, Leicester, 1977.

Eastlake, Charles, *Hints on Household Taste*, Longmans, Green and Co., London, 1868.

Edis, R.W., *The Decoration and Furniture of Town Houses*, 1881, reprinted by EP Publishing Limited, 1972, introduction by Christopher Gilbert.

Edwards, Ifor, *Decorative Cast Iron in Wales*, Gomer Press, Llandysul, 1989.

Elsam, Richard, *The Practical Builder's Perpetual Price Book*, Kelly, London, 1841, 1863 editions.

Ford, John, *Ackermann 1783–1983*, Arthur Ackermann Publishing Limited, London, 1983.

Franklin, J., *The Gentleman's Country House and its Plan, 1835–1914*, Routledge and Kegan Paul, London, 1981.

Gere, C., with Hoskins, L. *The House Beautiful: Oscar Wilde and the Aesthetic Interior*, Lund Humphries in association with The Geffrye Museum, London, 2000.

Girouard, Mark, *Sweetness and Light*, Yale University Press, New Haven and London, 1977.

Girouard, Mark, *The Victorian Country House*, Yale University Press, New Haven and London, 1979.

Gloag, John, *Mr Loudon's England*, Oriel Press Ltd, Newcastle, 1970.

Godwin, George, *Town Swamps and Social Bridges*, 1859, reprinted by Leicester University Press, 1972.

Gow, Ian, *The Scottish Interior*, Edinburgh University Press, Edinburgh, 1992.

Grier, Katherine C., *Culture and Comfort: People, Parlours and Upholstery 1850–1930*, The Strong Museum, University of Massachusetts Press, Mass. 1988.

Handlin, David P., *The American Home: Architecture and Society 1815–1915*, Little, Brown and Company, Boston, Mass, 1979.

Harris, Eileen, *British Architectural Books and Writers 1556–1785*, Cambridge University Press, 1990.

Harrison, Charles and Wood, Paul with Gaiger, Jason, *Art in Theory 1815–1900. An Anthology of Changing Ideas*, Blackwell Publishers Ltd, Oxford, 1998.

Haweis, Mrs H.R., *The Art of Decoration*, Chatto and Windus, London, 1889.

Hellyer, S.S., *The Plumber and Sanitary Houses*, Batsford, London, 1877.

Hinchcliffe, Tanis, *North Oxford*, Yale University Press, New Haven and London, 1992.

Hitchcock, Henry-Russell, *Early Victorian Architecture in Britain*, The Architectural Press, Yale University Press, New Haven and London, 1954.

Hobhouse, Hermione, *Thomas Cubitt Master Builder*, Management Books 2000 Ltd, 1995 edition.

Howe, Bea, *Arbiter of Elegance*, The Harvill Press, London, 1967 (about Mrs Haweis).

Humphrey, Repton, Dumbarton Oaks Research Library and Collection, Washington DC, 1994.

Hunter, Michael, *The Victorian Villas of Hackney*, Hackney Society, London, 1981.

Hyde, Matthew, *The Villas of Alderley Edge*, The Silk Press, Altrincham, 1999.

Jones, Edward and Woodward, Christopher, *A Guide to the Architecture of London*, Van Nostrand Reinhold Company, New York, 1983.

Jones, Owen, *The Grammer of Ornament*, 1856, reprinted by Studio Editions, London, 1986.

Kelly, Alison, *Mrs Coade's Stone*, The Self Publishing Association Ltd, Upton-on-Severn, Worcs, in conjunction with The Georgian Group, 1990.

Kerr, Robert, *The Gentleman's House*, John Murray, London, 1871.

Laxton, H., *The Builder's Price Book*, Kelly, London, 1826 and later editions.

Lewis, Philippa and Darley, Gillian, *Dictionary of Ornament*, Macmillan London Limited, London, 1986.

London Suburbs, Merrell Holberton, London, in association with English Heritage, 1999, introduction by Andrew Saint.

Long, Helen C., *The Edwardian House*, Manchester University Press, Manchester, 1993.

Loudon, John Claudius, *An Encyclopaedia of Cottage, Farm and Villa Architecture*, Longmans, London, 1833.

Loudon, John Claudius, *The Suburban Gardener and Villa Companion*, Longmans, London, 1838.

Lowe, J.B., *Welsh Industrial Workers Housing 1775–1875*, National Museum of Wales, Cardiff, 1977.

McMordie, Michael, 'Picturesque Pattern Books and Pre-Victorian Designers', *Architectural History* , 18, 1975, 43–59.

MacDougall, Elizabeth B., ed., *John Claudius Loudon and the Early Nineteenth Century in Great Britain*, Dumbarton Oaks, Washington DC, 1980.

Marzio, Peter C., *The Democratic Art*, David R Godine, Boston, 1979.

Millar, William, *Plastering Plain and Decorative*, Batsford, London, 1897.

Mintons Tiles Catalogue, 1885, reprinted by Richard Dennis Publications, Somerset, 1996, introduction by Chris Blanchett.

Mordaunt-Crook, J., *The Dilemma of Style*, John Murray, London, 1987.

Mumby, F.A. and Norrie, Ian, *Publishing and Bookselling*, Jonathon Cape, London, 5th edition revised 1974.

Murphy, Shirley Foster, *Our Homes and How to Make Them Healthy*, Cassell, London, 1883.

Muthesius, Hermann, *The English House*, reprinted by BSP Professional Books, Oxford, 1987.

Muthesius, Stefan, *The English Terraced House*, Yale University Press, New Haven and London, 1982.

Myles, Janet, *L.N Cottingham 1787–1847*, Lund Humphries Publishers, London, 1996.

Nicholson, Peter, *The New Practical Builder and Workman's Companion*, Kelly, London, 1823.

Panton, J., *From Kitchen to Garrett*, Ward and Downey, London, 1888.

Parker, Barry and Unwin, Raymond, *The Art of Building a Home*, Longmans, London, 1901.

Parker, Charles, *Villa Rustica*, James Carpenter and Son, London, 1832–41.

Pevsner, Nikolaus, Sir, *Some Architectural Writers of the Nineteeth Century*, Clarendon, Oxford, 1972.

Pictorial History of British Nineteenth Century Furniture Design, with an introduction by Edward Joy, Antique Collectors' Club, Suffolk, 1977.

Porter, Roy, *English Society in the Eighteenth Century*, Penguin Books Ltd, Middlesex, 1982.

Powell, C.G., *An Economic History of the British Building Industry 1815–1979*, Methuen, London and New York, 1982.

Pugin, A.W. N, *Contrasts,* 1836, reprinted by Leicester University Press, 1969, introduction by H-R.Hitchcock.

Reid, Aileen, *Brentham; A History of the Pioneer Garden Suburb 1901–2001*, Brentham Heritage Society, London, 2000.

Richardson, C.J. *Picturesque Designs for Mansions, Villas, Lodges etc*, Atchley, London, 1870.

Richardson, Ruth and Thorne, Robert, *The Builder Illustrations Index 1843–1883*, The Builder Group and Hutton and Rostron, in association with Institute of Historical Research, University of London, 1994.

Robertson, E. Graeme, and Robertson, Joan, *Cast Iron Decoration*, Thames and Hudson, London, 1994 edition.

Robinson, Peter Frederick, *Rural Architecture; Or, A Series of Designs for Ornamental Cottages*, 1823 and later editions.

Routh, Guy, *Occupations of the People of Great Britain, 1801–1981*, The Macmillan Press Ltd, London, 1987.

Rubenstein, David, *Victorian Homes*, David and Charles, Newton Abbot, 1974.

Ruskin, John, *The Seven Lamps of Architecture*, 1849, reprinted by Dover Publications, New York, 1989.

Ruskin, John, *The Stones of Venice*, 1851–3, reprinted by Penguin Books, London, 2001.

Saint, Andrew, *Richard Norman Shaw*, Paul Mellon Centre, Yale University Press, New Haven and London, 1976.

Sambrook, John, *Fanlights*, Chatto and Windus, London 1989.

Service, Alastair, *Edwardian Architecture*, Thames and Hudson, London, 1977.

Shaw, Henry, *Details of Elizabethan Architecture*, 1834.

Shaw, Richard Norman, *Sketches for Cottages and Other Buildings*, Lascelles, 1878.

Simo, M.L., *Loudon and the Landscape*, Yale University Press, New Haven and London, 1988.

Simpson, M.A. and Lloyd, T.H., *Middle Class Housing in Britain*, David and Charles, Newton Abbott, 1977.

Skinner, D.S. and van Lemmen, Hans, *Minton Tiles 1835–1935*, City Museum and Art Gallery, Stoke on Trent, 1984.

Snodin, Michael and Howard, Maurice, *Ornament; A Social History Since 1450*, Yale University Press, in association with Victoria and Albert Museum, New Haven and London, 1996.

Soros, Susan Weber, *E.W. Godwin: Aesthetic Movement Architect and Designer*, Yale University Press, New Haven and London, 1999.

Spain, Nancy, *Mrs Beeton and Her Husband*, Collins, London, 1948.

Stevenson, J. J., *House Architecture*, Macmillan, London, 1880.

Stratton, Michael, *The Terracotta Revival*, Victor Gollancz, London, 1993.

Summerson, John, ed., *Concerning Architecture:Essays on Architectural Writers and writing presented to Nikolaus Pevsner*, Allen Lane, London, 1968.

Summerson, John, *The Unromantic Castle*, Thames and Hudson, London, 1990.

Summerson, John, *Georgian London*, Penguin books, London, 1991.

Sutcliffe, G.L., *Principles and Practice of Modern House Construction*, Gresham, London, 1898.

[Tarbuck, E.L.], *The Builder's Practical Director*, Hagger, London, 1855–8.

Temple, Nigel, *John Nash and the Village Picturesque*, Alan Sutton, Gloucester, 1979.

The Victorian Cabinet-Maker's Assistant, Dover Publications, New York, 1970, introduction by John Gloag.

The Victorian Catalogue of Household Furnishing, Studio Editions, London 1994, introduced by Stephen Calloway.

The Victorian House Catalogue:Young and Marten, Sidgewick and Jackson, London 1990, foreword by Peter Howell.

Thorne, Robert, 'Building Bridges. George Godwin and Architectural Journalism', in Gordon Marsden (ed), *Victorian Values*, Longman, London, 1998, 116–26.

Thornton, Peter, *Authentic Decor, The Domestic Interior 1620–1929*, Weidenfeld and Nicholson, London, 1993.

Twyman, Michael, *The British Library Guide to Printing History and Techniques*, The British Library, London, 1998.

Walker, Philip, *The Victorian Catalogue of Tools for Trades and Crafts*, Studio Editions, London, 1994.

Walkling, Gillian, *Antique Bamboo Furniture*, Bell and Hyman Limited, London, 1979.

Webster, T., and Parkes, Mrs W., *An Encyclopaedia of Domestic Architecture*, London, 1844.

Weinreb, Ben and Hibbert, Christopher, eds, *The London Encyclopaedia*, Pan Macmillan Publishers Ltd, London, 1993 edition.

Wrightson, Priscilla, *The Small English House*, B. Weinreb Architectural Books Ltd., London, 1977.

Yeomans, David T., 'Early Carpenters' Manuals 1592–1820', *Journal of the Construction History Society*, volume 2, 1986, 13–33.

Index

Ackermann, Rudolph 12, 15, 25, 74,
    109
Adam, Robert 21
    Works in Architecture 21
Aesthetic movement 88, 92–93
Aquatint 15, 23
Architectural Association, foundation
    of 2
Architectural Library, The 12–13
Architectural Magazine, The 72
Architectural treatises 21
Architecture, formalization of
    profession 2
Arrowsmith, H.W. & A. 83
    *The House Decorator and Painters
        Guide* 83
'Art at Home' series 10, 92–93
Artisans and Labourers General
    Dwellings Company 3
Artists' houses 112
Arts and Crafts
    houses 8
    movement 116
Audsley, George Ashdown and
    William James 54, 56
    Cottage, Lodge and Villa Architecture
        54
    Polychromatic Decoration 54
Austin, William 3

Balconies 72
Balcony designs 102
Balluster designs 103
Barnard, Bishop and Barnard 100, 102,
    112, 114
Bartholomew, Alfred 78
    *Specifications for Practical
        Architecture* 78
Baths 107
Batsford 13
Bay window display 91
Bedford Park 8, 62, 64, 69, 113

Beeton's, Mrs *Book of Household
    Management* 89
Benn, J. Williams 116
    The Cabinet Maker 116
Bielefeld, Charles Frederick 98–99
Blackburne, Edward Lushington 52,
    81
    Suburban and Rural Architecture 52
    *The Mason's, Bricklayer's, Plasterer's
        and Decorator's Practical Guide*
        81
Blackie & Son 11, 13, 55, 74, 96
    The Cabinet-Maker's Assistant 74
    Villa and Cottage Architecture 55–59
Blaise Hamlet 61
Bogue, J.W. 49
    Domestic Architecture 49
Book production costs, cutting 13–14
Bookbinding 11
Booth, Charles 18
    Life and Labour of London 18
Brackets 83
Brick Tax, repeal of 42
Brickwork patterns 84
Brookes, S.H. 2, 40–41, 49, 68
    *Designs for Villa and Cottage
        Architecture* 2, 9, 40
    Rudimentary Treatise 67
Brown, Richard 41–42
    Domestic Architecture 41–42
Builder, The 15, 18, 45, 49, 50, 78,
    111–112
Builders Merchant, The 116
Builders
    as 'superior artisan' 2
    merchants 4, 104
Building
    Acts 76
    journals 18
    materials, supply of 3
    trades, growth of 3
    works, measuring 77–78

Building News, The 49, 50, 111–112, 114
Burn, Robert Scott 49, 81–82
  New Guide to Carpentry 81–82
  The Grammar of House Planning 49
  The New Guide to Masonry Bricklaying and Plastering 81

Cabinet Maker, The 116, 117, 118
Cardiff 9
Carpenters 4
Carpentry 81
  manuals 23
Cassell's
  Book of the Household 89–90, 95–96
  Household Guide 13
Cassell, John 13
Ceiling enrichments 73
Chambers, William 21
  Treatise on Civil Architecture 21
Cheap Wood Company, The 102
Chippendale, Thomas 97
Chromolithography 16–17, 43, 52, 99–100
Clarke, W.S. 2
Coadestone 98
Collis, James 1, 39–40
  The Builders' Portfolio of Street Architecture 1, 39–40
Continental influences 6
Copper plate engraving 13–14
Cornice designs 108, 116
Cottage orné 57
Cottingham, L.N. 71–72
  The Ornamental Metal Workers Director 71–72
Crunden, John 23
  Convenient and Ornamental Architecture 23
Cubitt, Thomas 2, 3
Curtain arrangements 89, 118
Cutler, Thomas 65, 66, 75
Cyfarthfa Castle 26

Davidson, E.A. 83
  House Painting, Graining and Marbling 83
Day, Lewis F. 13
Decorators 83
Doorways 103
Downing, A.J. 37, 49
Dresser, Christopher 75–76
  Studies in Design 75–76

Eastlake, Charles 90–92
  Hints on Household Taste 90–92
Edis, R.W. 93
Eighteenth century architectural books 11–12
Elizabethan style 33, 59
Elsam, Richard 77–78
  The Practical Builder's Perpetual Price Book 77–78
Engraving 14
Estates of houses 2

Family Economist, The 110
Fanlights 98
Fences 72
Firegrates 100, 114
Fireplaces 74, 90
Floor tiles 106
Foundations 88
Fountain design 109
Freake, Charles 3
Freizes 116
Furniture 73–74, 117

Gandy, J.M. 24
Garden design 35–36
Gardening 90, 91
Gate lodge design 30
Gates 101
Gibbs, James 21
  Book of Architecture 21
  Rules for Drawing the Five Orders 22
Goodwin, Francis 37
  Domestic Architecture 37–39
Gothic
  interior scheme 41
  Revival 9
  Revivalist Edmund Street 61
Gray, Charles 6
Great Exhibition of 1851: 98
Grecian mouldings 80
Grecian villa 30, 39, 58

Halfpenny, William 22
  Chinese and Gothick Architecture, Properly Ornamented 22
  New and Compleat System 22
  Practical Architecture 22
  Twelve Beautiful designs for Farmhouses 22
Hambridge, Charles 6
Hand colouring 14

Harding, J.D. 16, 28, 61

Haweis, Mrs 93

   The Art of Decoration 93

Hay, D.R. 83

Hellyer, S.S. 13, 87

Hibberd, Shirley 90

   *Rustic Adornments for Homes of
Taste* 90

Hine, Thomas 8

Home manuals 88–96

Hood, Charles 1

   *A Practical Treatise on Warming
Buildings* 1

Hope, Thomas 73–74

   *Household Furniture and Interior
Decoration* 73–74

Houses, numbers of 2, 4

Hullmandel, C.J. 15, 16, 28

Hunt, Thomas Frederick 31

   Exemplers of Tudor Architecture
31

Illustrated Carpenter and Builder 112,
114

Illustrations

   cost of 11

   techniques 13–18

Institute of British Architects,
foundation of 2

Interior

   decoration, first use of term
73–74

   fittings 72

International Health Exhibition of
1884: 88

Ironwork 71–72, 99–100

Italian

   lodge 54, 57

   villa 62

Italianate style 7, 37, 47, 65, 81

Jacobean style 6, 59

Japanese influence 75–76, 117

Jones, Owen 16–17

   The Grammar of Ornament 16

Journals 110–112

Kelly's price book 76, 77

Kendall, Henry 57

Kerr, Robert 50, 51

   12 principles of planning 52

   *The English Gentleman's Country
House* 50

Laing, David 24

Langley, Batty 22

   The Builder's Jewel 22

   *The City and Country Builders and
Workman's Treasury of Designs*
22

Lascelles, W.H. 62

   *Sketches for Cottages and Other
Buildings* 62

Laxton, William 77

Library, design for 30

Lithography 15–16

Loftie, W.J. 10, 11

   A Plea for Art in the Home 10

London 2–3, 6, 12, 22, 25, 46, 61, 67,
89, 93, 94

Loudon, Jane 90

   *Lady's Companion to the Flower
Garden* 90

Loudon, John Claudius 35–36, 38, 40,
72, 73–74, 111

   Architectural Magazine 39, 73, 111

   *Encyclopaedia of Cottage, Farm
and Villa Architecture* 36, 37, 52,
72, 74

   *The Suburban Gardener and Villa
Companion* 35–36

Louis XIV style 74

Lugar, Robert 26

   Villa Architecture 26

Macfarlane's

   catalogue 100

   designs 101, 102

   premises 101

Magazine publishing 109–110

   circulation 129

Mantel-piece shelves 92

Manuals, publishers of 13

Marvel, I. 61

   A Freehold Villa for Nothing 61

Millar, William 82

   Plastering Plain and Decorative 82

Mintons 99–100

Moorish furniture 117

Morris, Thomas 59, 60

   A House for the Suburbs 59

Morris, William 116

Moulding machine 4

Murphy, Shirley Foster 3, 62, 65, 88

Nash, John 4, 61, 72

Neoclassicism 73–74

Nesfield, Eden W. 61

   Specimens of Medieval Architecture
64

Nicholson, Peter 1, 78–80
  *A Treatise on Projection, with a
    Complete System of Isometric
    Drawing* 1
  The Carpenter's New Guide 78–79
  *The New Practical Builder and
    Workmen's Companion* 79
Norman 29, 31
Nottingham 8, 9
Numbers Trade 13, 73

Optimus valve closet 87
Ornament, Victorian 75–76
Ornaments 98
Osbourne House 32, 33

Pain, William 13, 23
Panton, Mrs 94–95
Paperhangings 105
Papier mâché designs 98–99
Papworth, J.B. 25
  Rural Residences 25
Parker and Unwin 2
  The Art of Building a Home 2, 69
Parker, Barry 69
Parker, Charles 31–32
  Villa Rustica 31–32
Parsonages 5
Periodical publishing 12
Plaster moulding 86
Plastering 82
Plaw, John 23, 24
  Rural Architecture and Design 23
Plumbing 87
Pocock, W.F. 72
  Modern Finishings for Rooms 72
Population in Victorian Britain 2
Price books 76–78
Price, Francis 23
Priestly and Weale 13
Print runs 12, 89–90
Publication titles, increase in demand
    for 11
Pugin, A.C. 34, 74, 109
  *A Series of Ornamental Timber
    Gables* 33
  Gothic Furniture 74
Pugin, A.W.N. 1, 33–35, 54, 61, 74
  Details of Antient Timber Houses 1,
    35
  Floriated Ornament 16–17
  *Gothic Furniture in the Style of
    the Fifteenth Cent* 35
  *True Principles of Pointed or Christian
    Architecture* 13, 33

Queen Anne houses 8, 61–62, 65, 67,
    75

Reading and writing, growth of 11
Ready-made components, availability
    of 4
Renaissance style 117
Repository of the Arts 109
Richardson, C.J. 1, 62
  Observations 1
  Picturesque Designs 61
Robinson, Peter Frederick 1, 8, 27, 28,
    31
  Designs for Ornamental Villas
    29
  *Domestic Architecture in the Tudor
    Style* 1
  Rural Architecture 27
Room schemes 94
Roumieu Gough, Charles and Hugh
    6
Ruling machines 14
Rural Italianate houses 6, 8, 31
Ruskin, John 42, 116
  The Seven Lamps of Architecture
    42
  The Stones of Venice 42

Samuel Hemming 47–48
  *Designs for Villas, Parsonages and
    Other Houses* 47–48
Sanitation and hygiene 88
Scotch Baronial 4
Scotch house design 56
Semi-detached houses 7, 115
Senefelder, Alois 15
Services of the house 49, 88
Shaw, Henry 16–17, 33, 34, 63, 64,
    72
  Details of Elizabethan Architecture
    33
  Encyclopaedia of Ornament 16–17
  Examples of Ornamental Metalwork
    72
Shaw, Richard Norman 61
Sheraton, Thomas 73
  Cabinet Dictionary 73
Small house design 113, 115
Soane, John 15
Spicer, John 3
Stained glass design 17
Stevenson, J.J. 65–67
  House Architecture 65
String courses 103
Subscription 12

Suburban
  houses 59
  design for garden 36
  small 2, 3
  villa, growth of 39–40
Suburbia, beginning of 2
Suburbs, early Victorian 5
Sutcliffe, G. Lister 88
  The Principles and Practice of Modern
    House Construction 88
Swags and panels 103
Swiss
  chalet 27, 31, 33, 35
  villa 8, 30, 53
Sylvia's Home Help Series 95–96

Talbert, Bruce J. 74
  Examples of Ancient and Modern
    Furniture 75
  Gothic Forms 75
Tarbuck, Edward Lance 43–45
  The Builder's Practical Director
    43–45
Taylor, I. & J. 12–13
Terracotta 102
Thomson, Alexander 58
Torquay 8
Trade catalogue for the building trades
  97–109
Trades, increase in new 3
Travel, effect on style 41–42
Tredgold, Thomas 80–81
  Elementary Principles of Carpentry
    80–81
Trendall, Edward William 35–36, 72
  Examples for Interior Finishings 72

Original Designs for Cottages and
  Villas 35–36
Truefitt, George 6, 7, 58
Tudor architecture 27, 31
Tudor style 5, 6, 27, 29

Unwin, Raymond 69

Verandahs 72
Victorian eclecticism 6
Victorian interiors, forming the look of
  73–74
Villa and cottage books 23, 26

Walsh, J.H. 89
  A Manual of Domestic Economy 89
Ware, Isaac 21
  A Complete Body of Architecture 21
Weale 13, 23, 46
  Designs and Examples of Cottages,
    Villas and Country Houses 46
Wedgewood 97
Whittock, Nathanial 82
  Painters and Glaziers Guide 82
Wickes, C. 47–49
Window
  gardening 91
  guards 72
Windows 114
Wood engraving 15
Woodworking machines 4
Wright, Julia McNair 10
  The Complete Home 10
Wyke, John 97

Young and Marten 17, 104, 106, 107